**TEACHER'S PET PUBLICATIONS**

LITPLAN TEACHER PACK
for
When the Legends Die
based on the book by
Hal Borland

Written by
Mary B. Collins

© 1996 Teacher's Pet Publications
All Rights Reserved

This **LitPlan** for Hal Borland's
When the Legends Die
has been brought to you by Teacher's Pet Publications, Inc.

Copyright Teacher's Pet Publications 1996
11504 Hammock Point
Berlin MD 21811

Only the student materials in this unit plan (such as worksheets, study questions, and tests) may be reproduced multiple times for use in the purchaser's classroom.

For any additional copyright questions,
contact Teacher's Pet Publications.

www.tpet.com

TABLE OF CONTENTS - *When the Legends Die*

Introduction	5
Unit Objectives	7
Reading Assignment Sheet	8
Unit Outline	9
Study Questions (Short Answer)	13
Quiz/Study Questions (Multiple Choice)	24
Pre-reading Vocabulary Worksheets	43
Lesson One (Introductory Lesson)	55
Nonfiction Assignment Sheet	58
Oral Reading Evaluation Form	60
Writing Assignment 1	57
Writing Assignment 2	64
Writing Assignment 3	70
Writing Evaluation Form	72
Vocabulary Review Activities	68
Extra Writing Assignments/Discussion ?s	66
Unit Review Activities	74
Unit Tests	77
Unit Resource Materials	113
Vocabulary Resource Materials	129

A FEW NOTES ABOUT THE AUTHOR
Hal Borland

Borland, Hal (1900-1978), U. S. author, born on May 14, 1900, in Sterling, Nebraska. Borland wrote books for young people before branching into novels for adults, essay, and other nonfiction. His work was renowned for its insightful perspective on the natural world.

Borland studied at the University of Colorado and Columbia University and then became a journalist, working as a reporter for the Denver Post and several other newspapers. He was a staff writer for the New York Times from 1937 to 1942, specializing in nature writing, and he contributed to Audobon Magazine between 1967 and 1978. Borland was awarded an honorary doctorate from the University of Colorado in 1944 and an Alumni Award from the Columbia School of Journalism in 1962. His books include such works for young readers as *Valor: The Story of a Dog* (1934), *Wapiti Pete: The Story of an Elk* (1938), and *The Youngest Shepherd* (1962); the autobiographical works *High, Wide and Lonesome* (1956) and *This Hill, This Valley* (1957); and the novels *The Seventh Winter* (1960) and *When the Legends Die* (1963). *High, Wide and Lonesome* won the Secondary Education Board annual book award and the Westerners Buffalo Award for best nonfiction in 1957. *When the Legends Die* was made into a motion picture in 1972 and was translated into nine languages.

Borland also wrote editorials, essays, and columns for many magazines and newspapers. His trademark unsigned editorials in The New York Times about seasonal changes in the country were collected in *Sundial of the Seasons* (1964) and *An American Year* (1973). Borland won the Meeman award for conservation writing in 1966 and the John Burroughs Medal for distinguished nature writing in 1968. He also wrote such nonfiction works as *Beyond Your Doorstep: A Handbook to the Country* (1962) and *The History of Wildlife in America* (1975). In 1977 his book of essays *The Golden Circle: A Book of Months* was awarded an Outstanding Science Books for Children award. Borland died on February 22, 1978 in Sharon, Connecticut.

INTRODUCTION - *When the Legends Die*

This unit has been designed to develop students' reading, writing, thinking, and language skills through exercises and activities related to *When the Legends Die* by Hal Borland. It includes sixteen lessons, supported by extra resource materials.

The **introductory lesson** introduces students to the themes of legends and dreams through a writing activity. Following the introductory activity, students are given a transition to explain how the activity relates to the book they are about to read. Following the transition, students are given the materials they will be using during the unit. At the end of the lesson, students begin the pre-reading work for the first reading assignment.

The **reading assignments** are approximately thirty pages each; some are a little shorter while others are a little longer. Students have approximately 15 minutes of pre-reading work to do prior to each reading assignment. This pre-reading work involves reviewing the study questions for the assignment and doing some vocabulary work for 8 to 10 vocabulary words they will encounter in their reading.

The **study guide questions** are fact-based questions; students can find the answers to these questions right in the text. These questions come in two formats: short answer or multiple choice. The best use of these materials is probably to use the short answer version of the questions as study guides for students (since answers will be more complete), and to use the multiple choice version for occasional quizzes. If your school has the appropriate equipment, it might be a good idea to make transparencies of your answer keys for the overhead projector.

The **vocabulary work** is intended to enrich students' vocabularies as well as to aid in the students' understanding of the book. Prior to each reading assignment, students will complete a two-part worksheet for approximately 8 to 10 vocabulary words in the upcoming reading assignment. Part I focuses on students' use of general knowledge and contextual clues by giving the sentence in which the word appears in the text. Students are then to write down what they think the words mean based on the words' usage. Part II nails down the definitions of the words by giving students dictionary definitions of the words and having students match the words to the correct definitions based on the words' contextual usage. Students should then have an understanding of the words when they meet them in the text.

After each reading assignment, students will go back and formulate answers for the study guide questions. Discussion of these questions serves as a **review** of the most important events and ideas presented in the reading assignments.

After students complete reading the work, there is a lesson devoted to the **extra discussion questions/writing assignments**. These questions focus on interpretation, critical analysis and personal response, employing a variety of thinking skills and adding to the students' understanding of the novel.

Following the discussion questions, there is a **vocabulary review** lesson which pulls together all of the fragmented vocabulary lists for the reading assignments and gives students a review of all of the words they have studied.

The **group activity** has students working in small groups to research and discuss several themes and ideas related to the ideas in the story. The group activity is followed by a **reports and discussion** session in which the groups share their research about the topics with the entire class; thus, the entire class is exposed to information about many different ideas related to the story.

There are three **writing assignments** in this unit, each with the purpose of informing, persuading, or having students express personal opinions. The first assignment is to express personal opinions: students write a composition in which they tell what the quotation, "When the legends die, the dreams end. When the dreams end, there is no more greatness" means. The second assignment is to inform: students write a composition in which they tell about the legends they read about, in preparation for an oral report. The third assignment is to practice persuasive writing: students choose an issue related to the environment, research it, and then write a letter to a government official persuading that person to agree with their own viewpoint.

The **nonfiction reading assignment** is combined with the third writing assignment in this unit. Students are required to read a piece of nonfiction related in some way to an issue about the environment. After reading their nonfiction pieces, students will fill out a worksheet on which they answer questions regarding facts, interpretation, criticism, and personal opinions, and then they will proceed with Writing Assignment #3.

The **review lesson** pulls together all of the aspects of the unit. The teacher is given four or five choices of activities or games to use which all serve the same basic function of reviewing all of the information presented in the unit.

The **unit test** comes in two formats: multiple choice or short answer. As a convenience, two different tests for each format have been included.

There are additional **support materials** included with this unit. The **unit resource** section includes suggestions for an in-class library, crossword and word search puzzles related to the novel, and extra vocabulary worksheets. There is a list of **bulletin board ideas** which gives the teacher suggestions for bulletin boards to go along with this unit. In addition, there is a list of **extra class activities** the teacher could choose from to enhance the unit or as a substitution for an exercise the teacher might feel is inappropriate for his/her class. **Answer keys** are located directly after the **reproducible student materials** throughout the unit. The student materials may be reproduced for use in the teacher's classroom without infringement of copyrights. No other portion of this unit may be reproduced without the written consent of Teacher's Pet Publications, Inc.

UNIT OBJECTIVES - *When the Legends Die*

1. Through reading *When the Legends Die*, students will study one man's search for his own identity as he struggles between two ways of life.

2. Students will consider the importance of one's own heritage.

3. Students will demonstrate their understanding of the text on four levels: factual, interpretive, critical and personal.

4. Students will be given the opportunity to practice reading aloud and silently to improve their skills in each area.

5. Students will answer questions to demonstrate their knowledge and understanding of the main events and characters in *When the Legends Die* as they relate to the author's theme development.

6. Students will enrich their vocabularies and improve their understanding of the novel through the vocabulary lessons prepared for use in conjunction with the novel.

7. The writing assignments in this unit are geared to several purposes:
   a. To have students demonstrate their abilities to inform, to persuade, or to express their own personal ideas
      Note: Students will demonstrate ability to write effectively to <u>inform</u> by developing and organizing facts to convey information. Students will demonstrate the ability to write effectively to <u>persuade</u> by selecting and organizing relevant information, establishing an argumentative purpose, and by designing an appropriate strategy for an identified audience. Students will demonstrate the ability to write effectively to <u>express personal ideas</u> by selecting a form and its appropriate elements.
   b. To check the students' reading comprehension
   c. To make students think about the ideas presented by the novel
   d. To encourage logical thinking
   e. To provide an opportunity to practice good grammar and improve students' use of the English language.

8. Students will read aloud, report, and participate in large and small group discussions to improve their public speaking and personal interaction skills.

READING ASSIGNMENT SHEET - *When the Legends Die*

Date Assigned	Chapters Assigned	Completion Date
	1-7	
	8-12	
	13-21	
	22-32	
	33-41	
	42-49	

UNIT OUTLINE - *When the Legends Die*

1 Introduction PV 1-7 Writing Assignment #1	2 Read 1-7	3 Study ?s 1-7 PVR 8-12	4 Study ?s 8-12 PVR 13-21 Research Activity	5 Library
6 Study ?s 13-21 PVR 22-32 Group Work	7 Study ?s 22-32 PVR 33-41	8 Study ?s 33-41 Writing Assignment 2 PVR 42-49	9 Study ?s 42-49 Research Reports	10 Research Reports
11 Extra Questions	12 Vocabulary	13 Writing Assignment 3	14 Sentence Structure Worksheet	15 Review
16 Test				

Key: P = Preview Study Questions V = Prereading Vocabulary Work R = Read

STUDY GUIDE QUESTIONS

SHORT ANSWER STUDY GUIDE QUESTIONS - *When the Legends Die*

Part I
1. Why did George and his family go to the mountains?
2. Who was Blue Elk?
3. Why did Charley Huckleberry and some of his tribe go to Horse Mountain? What trouble did their actions cause, and how was the problem resolved?
4. What was the problem about working at the sawmill and having credit at the store?
5. How did George and Bessie pay for the baptism?
6. Why did George kill Frank No Deer?
7. What is the "roundness"?
8. What was George's sign to Bessie?
9. Why did George check Bessie's path?
10. From where did the family's first meat come?
11. Why couldn't George get a deer the first time he tried?
12. Describe some of the "old ways" that George's family adopted.
13. How did George die?
14. How did the boy know the wailing song?
15. Why did they boy call himself "Bear's Brother"?
16. How did Bessie get a new axe?
17. What news did Jim Thatcher give to Bessie?
18. Why did Bessie make a second trip to Pagosa alone?
19. Why did Blue Elk steal Bessie's cloth?
20. How did Bessie die?
21. How did the boy come to have a bear cub as a pet?
22. Who saved the boy's cub in Pagosa?
23. Why did Blue Elk go into the woods to find the boy?
24. What did Blue Elk tell the boy about the old days?

Part II
1. Describe the Indians of Ignacio.
2. How did Blue Elk get "paid" for bringing the boy to Ignacio?
3. Identify Benny Grayback.
4. How did Thomas make room for his bear?
5. Describe how Thomas' bear was returned to the wild.
6. How did the trip to Horse Mountain change Thomas?
7. Why did the boys tease Thomas, calling him a girl?
8. What injustice did Neil do to Thomas?
9. Why did Thomas return to the school of his own free will after he escaped?
10. What happened when the bear returned to the school?

When the Legends Die - Study Guide page 2

11. How did the bear's return change Thomas?
12. What did Thomas think of plowing?
13. How did Thomas learn to ride wild colts?
14. Why was Thomas relieved of his horse-tending duties?
15. Identify Albert Left Hand.
16. Why did Thomas go to Bayfield, and what did he do there?

Part III
1. Identify Red Dillon.
2. Why did Red cut the straps on Thomas' saddle?
3. What was Red's scam?
4. Why was Thomas so mean to the horses?
5. Identify Meo.
6. How did Tom get a broken leg?
7. What was Red's response to Tom's broken leg?
8. What was Meo's response to Tom's broken leg?
9. What went wrong with Red's scam?
10. About what did Tom and Red argue?
11. What did Tom buy with the rodeo money?
12. What did the judge tell Tom?
13. What happened to Red?
14. Why did Tom have a losing streak?
15. Describe Tom's ride on Nightmare.
16. Why didn't Tom weed the garden after Meo died?
17. What did Tom do to the barn and cabin after Meo died?
18. How did Tom's riding style change?
19. Describe Tom's attitude towards life at this point in time.
20. Describe Tom's ride on Sky Rocket.
21. What were Tom's injuries from his ride on Sky Rocket?
22. Who was Mary Redmond?
23. Why was Mary upset with Tom?
24. Why wouldn't Tom go to Nyack?
25. What was Tom's only regret about Red?

When the Legends Die - Study Guide page 3

Part IV
1. Where did Tom go when he left the hospital?
2. Why did Tom need work clothes?
3. What job did Tom take to earn some money while his body finished healing?
4. What was strange about Mac to Tom?
5. Identify Charley.
6. How did Woodward find out that Tom was a rodeo rider?
7. Where did Tom plan to go after his job with Woodward was finished?
8. What frightened the sheep?
9. What was Tom's reaction to the bear?
10. Why did Tom wish he had not seen the bear's tracks?
11. Why did Tom go back to Horse Mountain to look for the bear?
12. Why didn't Tom kill the bear?
13. What was the All-Mother?
14. What did Tom say to the deer picture?
15. How did Tom change?

KEY: SHORT ANSWER STUDY GUIDE QUESTIONS - *When the Legends Die*

Part I

1. Why did George and his family go to the mountains?
    George killed Frank No Deer. He and his family fled to the mountains to get away from trouble.

2. Who was Blue Elk?
    Blue Elk was an Indian who acted as an interpreter and mediator between the Indians and the white people. He would do almost anything for a buck. He is the one who came with the sheriff to find George after the murder.

3. Why did Charley Huckleberry and some of his tribe go to Horse Mountain? What trouble did their actions cause, and how was the problem resolved?
    Charley Huckleberry took some members of his tribe to Horse Mountain to gather food for the winter. Their corn crops had failed during the hot summer drought, and the Indians needed food for the winter. The problem was that the Indians did not get permits to hunt on the land where they went. Blue Elk found the wayward members of the tribe and warned them of their trespasses. He said he could fix the situation by obtaining the necessary permits, and that he could arrange for jobs for the men so they could afford to buy the food they would need during the winter months.

4. What was the problem about working at the sawmill and having credit at the store?
    The Indians could never quite make enough to pay off their store debts, and they could not quit working as long as they had a debt at the store. Without careful planning, a person would have to work indefinitely at the sawmill.

5. How did George and Bessie pay for the baptism?
    George received an advance of one week's pay.

6. Why did George kill Frank No Deer?
    George had been working to save enough money to pay off the store debt so he would be free to leave the sawmill. Each time he had saved up a substantial amount of money, Frank No Deer stole the money. George killed him for stealing his money.

7. What is the "roundness"?
    The roundness describes the natural way of life; things in nature are round, as opposed to the things of man which are angular.

8. What was George's sign to Bessie?
    He left a willow twig in the moss.

9. Why did George check Bessie's path?
    He wanted to make sure that she had not been followed.

10. From where did the family's first meat come?
    George took it from the carcass of a mountain lion's catch.

11. Why couldn't George get a deer the first time he tried?
    Bessie said he missed because they had forgotten to sing the hunting song. Practically, though, George probably hadn't shot a bow and arrow since his childhood.

12. Describe some of the "old ways" that George's family adopted.
    They lived off of the land, hunting for their own food supply and making their clothes, tools, and other necessities from the plants and animals they found. They sang the old songs and lived in harmony with nature.

13. How did George die?
    He was killed in an avalanche while out hunting for meat.

14. How did the boy know the wailing song?
    He had not been taught that song; it was from his heart, a song known to man by instinct.

15. Why did the boy call himself "Bear's Brother"?
    He had made friends with a she-bear.

16. How did Bessie get a new axe?
    She went to Pagosa and traded her baskets for the axe at Jim Thatcher's store.

17. What news did Jim Thatcher give to Bessie?
    He said that the matter of the murder was settled, that George was no longer in trouble.

18. Why did Bessie make a second trip to Pagosa alone?
    She wanted reassurance that the trouble about the murder had been settled. She went alone because she worried that the boy might get caught and not be able to escape.

19. Why did Blue Elk steal Bessie's cloth?
    He said it was payment for his taking care of the murder problem; however, he didn't really have anything to do with the solving of that problem. He stole the cloth because it was worth money.

20. How did Bessie die?

    She was weak from hunger during the winter months, and she insisted on going on a hunting trip with the boy. She was far too weak, became ill, and died.

21. How did the boy come to have a bear cub as a pet?

    A stranger came and killed the she-bear and one of her cubs, leaving the other cub. The boy befriended the cub of his bear friend, and the cub responded.

22. Who saved the boy's cub in Pagosa?

    Jim Thatcher made everyone leave the cub alone.

23. Why did Blue Elk go into the woods to find the boy?

    The preacher hired him to do it. Because the preacher had baptized the boy, he felt a responsibility towards the boy since his parents were dead, so he sent Blue Elk to get the boy and take him to school.

24. What did Blue Elk tell the boy about the old days?

    He said that they were gone.

Part II

1. Describe the Indians of Ignacio.

    They dressed and acted like white men.

2. How did Blue Elk get "paid" for bringing the boy to Ignacio?

    The preacher paid him some money, saying that the agency would probably pay him more when he delivered they boy. However, the agency refused to pay, so Blue Elk went back to the boy's lodge, took everything of value, and burned down the rest.

3. Identify Benny Grayback.

    Benny was the carpentry instructor at the school, who was put in charge of Thomas' orientation to school life. He spoke Ute, but he behaved just like a white man, showing little or no understanding of the boy's point of view.

4. How did Thomas make room for his bear?

    He threw Luther Spotted Dog and his belongings out of the room.

5. Describe how Thomas' bear was returned to the wild.

    Blue Elk took Thomas and the bear to Horse Mountain. He chained the bear to a tree and told Thomas that he would leave the bear there to die unless Thomas would agree to send the bear home and to return to the school himself.

6. How did the trip to Horse Mountain change Thomas?
> Upon his return, he was more obedient and cooperative.

7. Why did the boys tease Thomas, calling him a girl?
> He took a basket weaving class and had long hair braids.

8. What injustice did Neil do to Thomas?
> Some boys were teasing Thomas in the barn. He got tired of it and beat them up. Neil came along and flogged Thomas for fighting.

9. Why did Thomas return to the school of his own free will after he escaped?
> When he returned to his lodge home, he found it was burned to the ground. He had lost his home and his friend. There was nothing left in the wild for him. He decided the old ways must be dead, so he returned to the school.

10. What happened when the bear returned to the school?
> Thomas was angry with the bear because it had not answered his call in the wild. He forgave the bear, though, and sent it off into the wild again for its own safety.

11. How did the bear's return change Thomas?
> He was more alone and more sad than ever before.

12. What did Thomas think of plowing?
> He thought it was senseless to try to make the land grow something that wasn't there naturally. He thought the land would do better left to its own ways, and that walking up and down rows was a waste of time since you didn't go anywhere with your walking.

13. How did Thomas learn to ride wild colts?
> Since he was a terrible farmer, the administrators at the school sent him out to tend to the wild horses. He wondered what it would be like to ride a wild horse, tried it, and eventually learned a way to master the animals.

14. Why was Thomas relieved of his horse-tending duties?
> The horses were growing thin. When Benny discovered _why_ they were thin (from being ridden and not allowed to graze), he changed Thomas' duties.

15. Identify Albert Left Hand.
> Thomas went to work for Albert Left Hand during the lambing season because the school didn't know what else to do with him. Albert was a slovenly, sullen man who did as little work as possible to get by.

16. Why did Thomas go to Bayfield, and what did he do there?
    He went to Bayfield with Albert to take the sheep to be shorn and to sell the pelts of the sheep that had died. From his experiences there, he realized two things: the work he did with his hands was worth money, and he could make money by riding horses.

Part III
1. Identify Red Dillon.
    In Bayfield Red discovered Thomas could ride, so he hired Thomas to work for him. Red was actually a hustler who used Thomas' riding skills as a way to make money for himself.

2. Why did Red cut the straps on Thomas' saddle?
    He cut the straps so that Thomas would learn to check his own gear himself and not to trust anyone else to do it for him.

3. What was Red's scam?
    He rode into town with Thomas, making people believe that Thomas was a kid who thought he could ride. He'd place small bets on Thomas in the early rounds, which Thomas would usually win, then he'd tell Thomas to lose in the finals. By losing the bets in the finals, he could then talk people into setting up a special event. Then, he would place large bets, and he would order Thomas to ride his best to win. In this way, he would collect large sums of money from the event.

4. Why was Thomas so mean to the horses?
    He was taking out his anger with Red on the horse.

5. Identify Meo.
    Meo was a Mexican who used to ride for Red in the same way that Tom was riding for him. After being forced to retire because of injuries, he cooked for Red and grew beans and chili peppers in a garden. Meo was friendly and sympathetic towards Tom, and he gave Tom good advice.

6. How did Tom get a broken leg?
    He rode a horse that crashed into a fence, crushing his leg between the horse and the fence.

7. What was Red's response to Tom's broken leg?
    He was furious because Tom couldn't ride for a while. That meant that Red would have no income for a while. Red went out and got drunk.

8. What was Meo's response to Tom's broken leg?
    He helped Tom as much as he could.

9. What went wrong with Red's scam?
   Tom was growing up and didn't look like a "little Indian kid" anymore. This made bettors wary.

10. About what did Tom and Red argue?
    Tom wanted to quit the scam and ride straight to win. Red wanted to continue the scam.

11. What did Tom buy with the rodeo money?
    He bought fancy clothes and a car, and got his hair cut.

12. What did the judge tell Tom?
    He said that Tom wouldn't make it to the big championships if he continued being so hard on himself and the horses.

13. What happened to Red?
    He became ill and died in a hotel room. His illness was mostly due to years of excessive drinking.

14. Why did Tom have a losing streak?
    He started riding for the crowd instead of concentrating on the ride itself.

15. Describe Tom's ride on Nightmare.
    Nightmare lunged and seemed to go crazy. The horse lunged into a gate, breaking it, then lunged again impaling itself with one of the broken boards and throwing Tom into the chute.

16. Why didn't Tom weed the garden after Meo died?
    He decided that the garden was Meo's, and Meo was gone. If the beans and peppers couldn't survive among the weeds, they didn't deserve to be there.

17. What did Tom do to the barn and cabin after Meo died?
    He burned them down.

18. How did Tom's riding style change?
    He started riding to punish the horse, to bring out the worst the horse could give, instead of riding clean for points. He didn't care whether he won or not; his ride was for the battle between himself and the horse.

19. Describe Tom's attitude towards life at this point in time.
    Tom outwardly appeared to be mad at the world. He didn't care about anything except those few moments when he was riding.

20. Describe Tom's ride on Sky Rocket.
> Tom tried to muscle Sky Rocket, and his leg went numb. In order to hold on, he dug his spurs into the horse's side, making the animal even more vicious. Tom jerked the animal's head, pulling the animal off balance. The animal fell, crushing Tom on the ground.

21. What were Tom's injuries from his ride on Sky Rocket?
> He had a punctured lung, a concussion, a broken pelvis, and a broken femur.

22. Who was Mary Redmond?
> She was a cheerful nurse who took exceptionally good care of Tom.

23. Why was Mary upset with Tom?
> He had walked before he was supposed to. She was afraid that he might damage his legs.

24. Why wouldn't Tom go to Nyack?
> Tom thought Mary was trying to run his life like Red, Blue Elk, and the others had done. He wanted to be independent.

25. What was Tom's only regret about Red?
> He regretted that Red had never seen him ride in the big circuit.

Part IV

1. Where did Tom go when he left the hospital?
> He went home to Pagosa.

2. Why did Tom need work clothes?
> He wanted to get a cheap room, but he was sure no one would give him a cheap room if he dressed in expensive clothes.

3. What job did Tom take to earn some money while his body finished healing?
> He became a sheep herder.

4. What was strange about Mac to Tom?
> Mac was a gentle horse; Tom hadn't ridden a gentle horse for quite a while.

5. Identify Charley.
> Charley was the supply man who came every Thursday. He was friendly but vulgar.

6. How did Woodward find out that Tom was a rodeo rider?
> He saw Tom's picture and an article in an old magazine.

7. Where did Tom plan to go after his job with Woodward was finished?
   He was going to go to Albuquerque to catch the rodeo circuit.

8. What frightened the sheep?
   A bear came, killed a lamb, and carried it off into the woods.

9. What was Tom's reaction to the bear?
   He chased it into the woods even though he had no weapon.

10. Why did Tom wish he had not seen the bear's tracks?
    The tracks were of a grizzly bear, like the one he had when he was a boy. The tracks brought back memories of his mother and his past.

11. Why did Tom go back to Horse Mountain to look for the bear?
    The bear was the one last remaining thing from his past to remind him he was an Indian. He wanted to kill the bear and make a clean break from his past.

12. Why didn't Tom kill the bear?
    His ancestral ties with nature deep within him would not let him kill the bear just for the sake of killing. The bear had done nothing to harm him. To have killed the bear would have been to completely go against all of his instincts and the beliefs he had held for so long. He could not make a total break with the past.

13. What was the All-Mother?
    The All-Mother was a vision Tom had, a woman who represented all of the mothers and grandmothers back to the beginning of time.

14. What did Tom say to the deer picture?
    He apologized for killing her sister and wasting the meat. He promised to make use of every part of the next deer he would kill.

15. How did Tom change?
    He began to live his life in the old way once more, realizing that he could not hide from his roots, he could not change who he was. Instead of fighting to put the past away, he faced it and accepted it as a part of his life.

MULTIPLE CHOICE STUDY GUIDE/QUIZ QUESTIONS - *When the Legends Die*

Part I

1. Why did George and his family go to the mountains?
    a. They were going on a fishing trip to one of George's favorite streams.
    b. George killed Frank No Deer. He and his family fled to get away from trouble.
    c. They owed money to the company store and were not able to pay. They went to the mountains to trap furs to use in exchange for payment of their debt.
    d. Bessie was sick. George knew of an old medicine man who lived alone in the mountains. He took her there hoping she would be cured.

2. Which of the following statements does not describe Blue Elk?
    a. He is George's brother-in-law.
    b. He acted as interpreter and mediator between the Indians and the white people.
    c. He would do almost anything for money.
    d. He came with the sheriff to find George.

3. Why did Charley Huckleberry and some of his tribe go to Horse Mountain?
    a. They were visiting a sacred burial ground because the eldest member of their tribe had died and they wanted to conduct a traditional, ritualistic burial.
    b. Charley wanted to make sure the youngsters knew how to survive in the wild.
    c. They went to capture some wild ponies that they wanted to tame and use for transportation.
    d. They went to gather food for the winter. Their corn crop had failed, and they needed food, so they went hunting.

4. True or false: Blue Elk found the Indians and warned them that they were trespassing. He said he could arrange the necessary permits. He offered to get them jobs so they could afford to buy food.
    a. True
    b. False

5. True or False: The Indians who worked at the sawmill were able to make enough money to pay off their store debts and quit working in only a few months.
    a. True
    b. False

6. How did George and Bessie pay for the baptism?
    a. Their friends all donated money.
    b. They borrowed it from Blue Elk.
    c. George received an advance of one week's pay.
    d. Bessie did some extra housecleaning and made enough to cover the costs.

When the Legends Die Multiple Choice Study Questions Page 2

7. Why did George kill Frank No Deer?
    a. Frank had been making advances to Bessie and George was jealous.
    b. George was drunk. They got into a fist fight about who was stronger and George beat him to death.
    c. Some of the white men wanted Frank out of the way because he was a bad influence. They offered George a large sum of money to do the job. He saw it as an opportunity to get enough money to buy his way out of the sawmill.
    d. Three different times George had saved enough money to pay off his store debt. Each time, Frank stole the money. The third time Frank stole the money, George killed him.

8. What was the natural way of life called?
    a. It was called "the healing".
    b. It was called "the yin-yang."
    c. It was called "the roundness."
    d. It was called "the earth cycle."

9. What was George's sign to Bessie?
    a. He left a willow twig in the moss.
    b. He left a notch carved on the trunk of a poplar tree.
    c. He left some seed scattered on the ground.
    d. He left a bouquet of wildflowers next to the path.

10. True or False: George checked Bessie's path because he did not trust her. He did not believe that a woman could really travel through the woods successfully on her own.
    a. True
    b. False

11. From where did the family's first meat come?
    a. Bessie brought it from home.
    b. George killed a deer.
    c. They stole it from a trapper's camp.
    d. George took it from the carcass of a mountain lion's catch.

12. True or False: George couldn't get a deer the first time he tried because he needed glasses. He wasn't able to focus correctly to kill it.
    a. True
    b. False

When the Legends Die Multiple Choice Study Questions Page 3

13. Which of the following is not one of the "old ways" the family adopted?
    a. They hunted for their own food.
    b. They made their own clothes and tools from plants and animals.
    c. They offered live sacrifices to the Great Spirit.
    d. They sang the old songs.

14. How did George die?
    a. He was killed in an avalanche while out hunting for meat.
    b. He was bitten by a rattlesnake.
    c. He stepped into a hunter's trap. He managed to get loose, but the wound got infected. Eventually he got gangrene and died.
    d. He was killed by an angry bear.

15. How did the boy know the wailing song?
    a. His mother taught him.
    b. He had learned it in school.
    c. He knew it by instinct.
    d. His father had taught him.

16. What did the boy call himself?
    a. He called himself "Bear's Brother."
    b. He called himself "Lone Wolf."
    c. He called himself "Earth Boy."
    d. He called himself "Moon Dancer."

17. How did Bessie get a new axe?
    a. She stole it from a house in town.
    b. She traded some of her baskets for it in town.
    c. She sneaked back to their old house and got it.
    d. She found an old friend and asked her to get it.

18. What news did Bessie receive from Jim Thatcher?
    a. He said that the matter of the murder was settled, and George was no longer in trouble.
    b. He said that George was still wanted, and the punishment would extend to his son.
    c. He said she would have to pay for George's crime.
    d. He said she would have to give up her land.

When the Legends Die Multiple Choice Study Questions Page 4

19. True or False: Bessie took her son with her on the second trip to Pagosa. She wanted him to protect her from any trouble in town.
    a. True
    b. False

20. Why did Blue Elk steal Bessie's cloth?
    a. He said she had stolen it from him and he was just getting it back.
    b. He said it was his payment for taking care of the murder problem.
    c. He said George owed him money from a gambling debt.
    d. He was drunk and was making advances to her. When she refused him, he got angry and took her cloth. He said he wouldn't give it back unless she gave in to him. She refused, and he left with the cloth.

21. How did Bessie die?
    a. She had a burst appendix.
    b. She ate some tainted meat.
    c. She was weak from hunger, but insisted on going on a hunting trip. She was too weak, became ill, and died.
    d. She was climbing a rocky ledge to get some eggs from a nest. She lost her footing and fell. Eventually she died of internal bleeding.

22. How did the boy come to have a bear cub as a pet?
    a. A stranger came and killed the she-bear and one cub, leaving the other cub.
    b. The mother and the other cub ran away when they heard a mountain lion coming. The smaller cub wasn't quick enough and the mountain lion attacked. The boy shot the lion and saved the cub.
    c. The boy found the cub wandering around in the woods. Since there was no sign of a mother, he kept it.
    d. The bear cub attacked the boy's camp. The boy was able to subdue the cub by offering it food and singing the bear song to it.

23. Who saved the boy's cub in Pagosa?
    a. The preacher saved it.
    b. Blue Elk saved it.
    c. Jim Thatcher saved it.
    d. The boy's uncle saved it.

When the Legends Die Multiple Choice Study Questions Page 5

24. Why did Blue Elk go to the woods to find the boy?
    a. He was the boy's godfather, and felt it was his responsibility to protect the boy.
    b. He wanted to bring the boy home as a servant, since he had no family of his own.
    c. He wanted to live the old way with the boy.
    d. The preacher hired him to do it.

25. What did Blue Elk tell the boy?
    a. He said he would only have to stay at the school for six months.
    b. He said the boy's parents had wanted him to go to the school, but couldn't afford it.
    c. He said the old days were gone.
    d. He said the boy could live the new way at the school and then go to the woods and live the old way in the summer.

When the Legends Die Multiple Choice Study Questions Page 6
Part II
26. Describe the Indians of Ignacio.
    a. They dressed and acted like white men.
    b. They dressed and lived in the "old way."
    c. They dressed like white men but lived in the "old way."
    d. They dressed in the "old way" but acted like white men.

27. True or False: The preacher paid Blue Elk some money for bringing the boy to Ignacio. Blue Elk expected more money from the agency, but they refused to pay. Blue Elk then went to the boy's lodge, took everything of value, and burned down the rest.
    a. True
    b. False

28. True or False: Benny Grayback was the headmaster at the school. He spoke Ute, and was very understanding of the boys" point of view.
    a. True
    b. False

29. How did Thomas make room for his bear?
    a. He built a lodge in the woods behind the school.
    b. He took over part of the basement.
    c. He was given space in the barn.
    d. He threw Luther Spotted Dog and his belongings out of their room.

30. True or False: Blue Elk and Thomas took the bear to Horse Mountain. When Thomas saw how the bear seemed to enjoy the open space, he realized that it was best to let the bear go.
    a. True
    b. False

31. How did the trip to Horse Mountain change Thomas?
    a. He became even more sullen and uncooperative.
    b. He became very depressed, and stopped eating and attending classes.
    c. He became obedient and cooperative.
    d. He became a model student, and made many friends.

32. Why did the boys tease Thomas and call him a girl?
    a. He had a high voice and delicate hands.
    b. He was not athletic and didn't enjoy sports.
    c. He preferred reading and cooking to the shop classes.
    d. He took a basket weaving class and had long hair in braids.

When the Legends Die Multiple Choice Study Questions Page 7

33. True or False: Neil supported Thomas' right to defend himself from the boys who were teasing him.
    a. True
    b. False

34. True or False: Thomas returned to the school after his escape because after he found his lodge destroyed, he decided the old ways must be dead.
    a. True
    b. False

35. What happened when the bear returned to school?
    a. Thomas kept it at the school.
    b. Thomas sent it off into the wild again for its own safety.
    c. An angry farmer shot it.
    d. It attacked the teacher.

36. How did the bear's return change Thomas?
    a. He was more vocal about remembering the old ways.
    b. He was happier than he had ever been.
    c. He became very studious.
    d. He was more alone and sad than ever before.

37. What did Thomas think of plowing?
    a. He enjoyed being so close to the land, getting out in the fresh air and sunshine for exercise, and having the opportunity to see things grow.
    b. He thought it was senseless to try to make the land grow something that wasn't there naturally, and plowing was a waste of time because you didn't go anywhere.

38. True or False: While tending the wild horses, Thomas tried to ride them, and eventually learned a way to master the horses.
    a. True
    b. False

39. Why was Thomas relieved of his horse-tending duties?
    a. The school administrators decided to have him make baskets to sell for profit.
    b. He spent all of his time daydreaming, and a couple of the horses got away.
    c. Mr. Swanson's nephew wanted the job, so Thomas was removed.
    d. Benny discovered that Thomas was riding the horses and keeping them thin instead of fattening them up.

When the Legends Die Multiple Choice Study Questions Page 8

40. Identify Albert Left Hand.
    a. He was an energetic, cheerful man who was a good influence on Thomas.
    b. He was a slovenly, sullen man who did as little work as possible.
    c. He was the tribe's medicine man.
    d. He was a man who had been attacked by a bear and had lost his right hand.

41. Why did Thomas go to Bayfield?
    a. H wanted to buy a new coat.
    b. He wanted to get a job there.
    c. He went to get the sheep shorn and sell the pelts of the sheep that had died.
    d. Albert offered to take him there and "show him the town."

42. What did he discover?
    a. He found out that not all whites treated the Indians badly.
    b. He found out that the work he did with his hands was worth money, and he could make money by riding horses.
    c. He found out that there was a group of Indians who were practicing the old ways, and he was invited to join their community.
    d. He found out that Albert was cheating the school out of some of the profit from the sheep. Albert threatened to kill him if he told.

When the Legends Die Multiple Choice Study Questions Page 9

Part III
43. Identify Red Dillon.
    a. He was a hustler.
    b. He was a cattle rancher.
    c. He was a horse breeder.
    d. He was a gambler.

44. What did Red do to Thomas?
    a. He put burrs under the saddle to see if Thomas could really ride.
    b. He gave him the meanest horse to ride first while he was fresh and had a lot of energy.
    c. He tied Thomas' hand to the saddle horn to make sure he stayed on the horse.
    d. He cut the straps on the saddle so Thomas would learn to check his own gear.

45. Which of the following was not part of Red's scam?
    a. He placed small bets on Thomas in the early rounds.
    b. He made Thomas lose in the finals.
    c. He told people that Tom had never ridden in a rodeo before.
    d. He talked people into setting up a special event.

46. What was Thomas' attitude with regard to the horses?
    a. He was taking out his anger with Red on the horses.
    b. He treated them the way he had treated the bear; like brothers.
    c. He was afraid of their spirits.
    d. He was indifferent towards them.

47. Which of the following statements does not describe Meo.
    a. He was a Pawnee Indian.
    b. He was a former rider who had been sidelined due to injuries.
    c. He cooked for Red and grew beans and chili peppers.
    d. He was friendly and sympathetic towards Tom.

48. How did Tom get a broken leg?
    a. He rode a horse that crashed into a fence, crushing his leg between the horse and the fence.
    b. He was lying on his back under the wagon, fixing a broken axle. When he hammered on a rod, it shook the supports and the wagon fell on his leg.
    c. He jumped from the fence and landed at an awkward angle. The force of the fall broke his leg.
    d. He was drunk and went out for a walk. He tried to climb up a steep hill and fell.

When the Legends Die Multiple Choice Study Questions Page 10

49. What was Red's response to Tom's broken leg?
    a. He offered sympathy and told Tom to stay in bed.
    b. He was indifferent and made no response.
    c. He told Tom that any doctor bills would have to come from his salary.
    d. He was furious because he was losing income while Tom was recuperating. He went out and got drunk.

50. What was Meo's response to Tom's broken leg?
    a. He ignored Tom, saying he was too busy to care for him.
    b. He offered to care for Tom for the fee of two dollars per day.
    c. He offered as much help as he could.
    d. He ridiculed Tom for his carelessness and suggested he find a place in town to stay until he was well again.

51. What happened with Red's scam?
    a. Some of the bettors traveled from town to town. They began to recognize Tom and tell their friends not to bet on him.
    b. Tom was growing up and didn't look like a little kid anymore. This made the bettor wary.
    c. The sheriff caught on to the scam and threw Red in jail.
    d. Red and Tom got filthy rich and decided to quit the scam while they were ahead of the game.

52. About what did Tom and Red argue?
    a. Tom wanted more money, a full fifty percent of the take. Red only wanted to give him 10%.
    b. Red wanted Tom to ride every day. Tom wanted to ride every two or three days, so that he could rest in between.
    c. Tom wanted to quit the scam and ride straight to win. Red wanted to continue the scam.
    d. Red wanted Tom to bill himself as "Injun Tom, the Horsebreaker." Tom didn't want to refer to himself that way.

53. Which of the following was not one of the things Tom did with his rodeo money?
    a. He bought a new cooking pot for Meo.
    b. He bought new clothes.
    c. He bought a car.
    d. He got his hair cut.

When the Legends Die Multiple Choice Study Questions Page 11

54. What did the judge tell Tom?
    a. The judge told Tom that Indians were not allowed to ride in the big championships.
    b. The judge told Tom that he was getting a reputation for dishonesty and should dump Red and go out on his own.
    c. The judge told Tom he had a lot of potential and should develop it.
    d. The judge told him he wouldn't make it to the big championships if he continued being so hard on himself and the horses.

55. What happened to Red?
    a. He was thrown from a horse and broke his neck.
    b. He became ill from excessive drinking and died in a hotel room.
    c. He went back East to live with his sister. He died shortly after he reached her home.
    d. He was shot and killed in a bar room brawl.

56. Why did Tom have a losing streak?
    a. He was depressed about Red's death and couldn't concentrate.
    b. He was suffering from pneumonia and wasn't taking care of himself.
    c. He was just getting bad horses; there wasn't anything he could do about it.
    d. He started riding for the crowd instead of concentrating on the ride itself.

57. Which of the following did not happen during Tom's ride on Nightmare?
    a. The horse bit him.
    b. The horse lunged into a gate.
    c. The horse impaled itself on a broken board.
    d. Tom was thrown into the chute.

58. Why didn't Tom weed the garden after Meo died?
    a. He thought it was work for women and old men.
    b. He was too busy practicing his riding.
    c. He decided the garden was Meo's. If the beans and peppers couldn't survive among the weeds, they didn't deserve to be there.
    d. He didn't like beans or peppers, so he had no motivation to care for them.

59. What did Tom do to the barn and cabin after Meo died?
    a. He painted them, repaired them, and sold them at a good profit.
    b. He burned them down.
    c. He cleaned them, bought new furniture and moved in.
    d. He left them the way they were as a memorial.

When the Legends Die Multiple Choice Study Questions Page 12

60. What happened to Tom's riding style?
    a. It stayed the same.
    b. It became more gentle because he was more in tune with the horses.
    c. He became more concerned with show and began riding for the approval of the crowds.
    d. He began to punish the horses, to bring out the worst in them.

61. Describe Tom's attitude towards life at this point.
    a. He outwardly appeared to be mad at the world.
    b. He seemed depressed and lethargic.
    c. He was the most outgoing he had ever been.
    d. It wasn't any different than it had been; he didn't seem to be capable of personal growth.

62. Which of the following did not happen during Tom's ride on Sky Rocket?
    a. His leg went numb.
    b. He dug his spurs into the horse's side, making it more vicious.
    c. Tom jerked the reins and the animal reared on its two hind legs, causing Tom to tear a muscle in his shoulder.
    d. The horse fell, crushing Tom on the ground.

63. Which of the following was not one of Tom's injuries from his ride on Sky Rocket?
    a. He had a punctured lung.
    b. He had a concussion.
    c. He had a ruptured spleen.
    d. He had a broken femur.

64. Who was Mary Redmond?
    a. She was a fan who came to visit Tom in the hospital.
    b. She was a cheerful nurse who took care of Tom.
    c. She was the rodeo owner's wife.
    d. She was an official from the Health and Safety Administration.

65. True or False: Mary was upset with Tom because he had walked before he was supposed to.
    a. True
    b. False

66. Did Tom go to Nyak?
    a. Yes. He liked the thought of being taken care of for once in his life.
    b. No. He didn't want anyone else to run his life.

When the Legends Die Multiple Choice Study Questions Page 13

67. What was Tom's only regret about Red?
    a. He was sorry that Red had never seen him ride in the big circuit.
    b. He was sorry that Red didn't get a church burial.
    c. He was sorry that he had not asked for more of the money when Red was alive, instead of allowing Red to spend it on liquor.
    d. He was sorry he didn't try to help Red find a wife and settle down.

When the Legends Die Multiple Choice Study Questions Page 14

Part IV

68. Where did Tom go when he left the hospital?
    a. He went to Nyack.
    b. He went to Pagosa.
    c. He went to Arboles.
    d. He went to Aztec.

69. Why did Tom need work clothes?
    a. His rodeo clothes were all torn and dirty and he looked like a bum. He didn't think he looked reputable enough for anyone to offer him a job.
    b. He was wearing expensive clothes. He was sure no one would rent him a cheap room while he was dressed the way he was.
    c. His clothes were practically rags. He needed sturdier clothes to protect him from the sun and the brambles along the trail.
    d. Someone stole his clothes while he was bathing. He had borrowed some trowsers and a shirt, but he needed to get some clothes of his own.

70. What job did Tom take to earn some money while his body finished healing?
    a. He wove baskets and sold them to the general store and to tourists.
    b. He gave horseback riding lessons.
    c. He became a dishwasher in a small restaurant.
    d. He became a sheep herder.

71. True or False: Tom thought it was strange to ride a gentle horse like Mac.
    a. True
    b. False

72. Who is Charley?
    a. He is the owner of the general store.
    b. He is the owner of the ranch where Tom is working.
    c. He is another sheep herder Tom met on the trail.
    d. He is the supply man who came once a week.

73. How did Woodward find out Tom was a rodeo rider?
    a. Tom told him.
    b. He had been to some of the rodeos and recognized Tom.
    c. He saw Tom's picture and an article in an old magazine.
    d. Someone in town recognized Tom and spread the news around.

When the Legends Die Multiple Choice Study Questions Page 15

74. Where did Tom plan to go after his job with Woodward was finished?
    a. He was going to settle down in Pagosa and raise horses.
    b. He was going back to the reservation to help his people remember the old ways.
    c. He was going to Albuquerque to catch the rodeo circuit.
    d. He was going to go back to New York to visit Mary.

75. True or False: A bear came, killed a lamb, and frightened the sheep.
    a. True
    b. False

76. What was Tom's reaction to the incident?
    a. He was afraid of the animal.
    b. He thought the animal was only doing what its nature intended, and he left it alone.
    c. He tried to capture it.
    d. He chased it into the woods even though he had no weapon.

77. How did Tom feel about seeing the bear's tracks?
    a. He was glad to see that there were still bears in the area.
    b. It made him sad, because it reminded him of the bear he had as an Indian child.
    c. The tracks made him fearful.
    d. It made him angry, though his anger was misplaced just as it had been in the earlier incident with the horses.

78. Why did Tom go back to Horse Mountain to look for the bear?
    a. He wanted to kill it and make a clean break from his past.
    b. He thought it was his childhood bear. He wanted to try and tame it again.
    c. He was just curious to see if it was, indeed, the same bear he had known as a child.
    d. It had to be destroyed so it would not attack people any more. Someone had to kill it, and Tom felt a certain obligation to the task.

79. Did Tom do as he originally intended?
    a. Yes, he did.
    b. No, he didn't.

80. Tom had a vision of a woman. Who was it?
    a. It was his mother.
    b. It was the All-Mother.
    c. It was the Earth Spirit.
    d. It was The Goddess of the Woods.

When the Legends Die Multiple Choice Study Questions Page 16

81. What did Tom say to the deer picture?
    a. He apologized for killing her sister and wasting the meat. He promised to make use of every part of the next deer he would kill.
    b. He thanked the deer for the delicious meat and said he hoped she didn't feel too much pain from the bullet.
    c. He was disrespectful and said it was the deer's lot in life to be eaten by man, who was more powerful.
    d. He didn't say anything. He thought the old way of talking to animal spirits was foolish.

82. True or False: Tom began to live his life in the old way once more, realizing that he could not hide from his roots, could not change who he was.
    a. True
    b. False

ANSWER KEY - MULTIPLE CHOICE STUDY/QUIZ QUESTIONS
When the Legends Die

Part I	Part II	Part III	Part IV
1. B	26. A	43. A	68. B
2. A	27. A	44. D	69. B
3. D	28. B	45. C	70. D
4. C	29. D	46. A	71. A
5. B	30. B	47. A	72. D
6. C	31. C	48. A	73. C
7. D	32. D	49. D	74. C
8. C	33. B	50. C	75. A
9. A	34. A	51. B	76. D
10. B	35. B	52. C	77. B
11. D	36. D	53. A	78. A
12. A	37. A	54. D	79. B
13. C	38. A	55. B	80. B
14. A	39. C	56. D	81. A
15. C	40. B	57. A	82. A
16. D	41. C	58. C	
17. B	42. B	59. B	
18. A		60. D	
19. B		61. A	
20. B		62. C	
21. C		63. C	
22. A		64. B	
23. B		65. A	
24. D		66. B	
25. C		67. A	

PREREADING VOCABULARY WORKSHEETS

VOCABULARY - *When the Legends Die*

<u>Chapters 1-7</u> Part I: Using Prior Knowledge and Contextual Clues

Below are the sentences in which the vocabulary words appear in the text. Read the sentence. Use any clues you can find in the sentence combined with your prior knowledge, and write what you think the underlined words mean on the lines provided.

1. She clapped a hand to her mouth to <u>stifle</u> the cry of hurt and surprise.

_____

2. Twice more they stopped to rest. The boy's legs were <u>weary</u>.

_____

3. But it had gone back to a den on a high ledge and would sleep, <u>sated,</u> all that day.

_____

4. . . . she wove a basket from willow stems and filled it with the meal and <u>leached</u> it sweet with water from the stream.

_____

5. She went outside and saw the <u>plume</u> of fine snow that is like a cloud over a big slide

_____

6. She <u>beckoned</u> to the boy, and together they looked about the store.

_____

Part II: Determining the Meaning - Match the vocabulary words to their dictionary definitions.

    ___ 1. stifle   A. Tired
    ___ 2. weary   B. Remove soluble parts by running water over or through a substance
    ___ 3. sated   C. A feather-like form, structure or object
    ___ 4. leached   D. Hold back; suppress; repress
    ___ 5. plume   E. Summoned by using gestures
    ___ 6. beckoned   F. Completely filled or satisfied

Vocabulary - *When the Legends Die*   Chapters 8-12

Part I: Using Prior Knowledge and Contextual Clues

Below are the sentences in which the vocabulary words appear in the text. Read the sentence. Use any clues you can find in the sentence combined with your prior knowledge, and write what you think the underlined words mean on the lines provided.

7. He said, "This is too much," and he put a hand on what she had chosen. They haggled. Finally he said, "You are a smart woman, Bessie. . . ."

_____

8. She smiled, depreciating.

_____

9. The cubs wanted to listen, but she cuffed them and told them not to listen.

_____

10. . . . broke open a box of cartridges and jammed three of them into the magazine. He levered one into the chamber as he hurried to the door . . . .

_____

11. He saw the tanned robes hung along the walls, the new buckskin folded carefully, the sewing basket with its coil of dry sinew and its bone awls.

_____

12. There was a coil of strips in a bowl of water, pliant for weaving

_____

Part II: Determining the Meaning - Match the vocabulary words to their dictionary definitions.

___ 7. haggled		A. Slapped
___ 8. depreciating		B. Bargained; argued over terms
___ 9. cuffed		C. Tendons
___ 10. levered		D. Belittling; making less of something
___ 11. sinew		E. Bendable
___ 12. pliant		F. Pushed as if using a lever

Vocabulary - *When the Legends Die* Chapters 13-21

Part I: Using Prior Knowledge and Contextual Clues

    Below are the sentences in which the vocabulary words appear in the text. Read the sentence. Use any clues you can find in the sentence combined with your prior knowledge, and write what you think the underlined words mean on the lines provided.

13. A moment later Blue Elk came in, all smiles and <u>expectancy</u>.

_____

14. "No," Benny said. "You are staying here." He <u>pinioned</u> the boy's arms.

_____

15. Luther looked at Thomas, <u>dubious</u>, but he said, "Yes."

_____

16. . . . and there still were things in them that he could not <u>fathom</u>.

_____

17. Ed, a half-blood, was an easygoing man with none of Benny's <u>zeal</u> to cancel Thomas Black Bull's background and inheritance overnight.

_____

18. . . . had whispered among themselves about how handsome he was in a rather <u>sullen</u> way. . . .

_____

19. He . . .took a butcher knife, a ball of strong cord and the two-pound <u>remnant</u> of a potroast.

_____

20. The boys who had <u>taunted</u> him now left him alone.

_____

Legends Vocabulary Chapters 13-21 Continued

21. Albert Left Hand was a short, fat man who smelled of <u>rancid</u> mutton tallow.

_____

22. In the window was the most beautiful saddle he had ever seen <u>ornately</u> tooled and polished

_____

Part II: Determining the Meaning
    Match the vocabulary words to their dictionary definitions. If there are words for which you cannot figure out the definition by contextual clues and by process of elimination, look them up in a dictionary.

___ 13. expectancy	A.	Sulky; moody
___ 14. pinioned	B.	Teased; mocked
___ 15. dubious	C.	Doubtful
___ 16. fathom	D.	Restrained by restricting one's arms
___ 17. zeal	E.	Something left over
___ 18. sullen	F.	Rotten
___ 19. remnant	G.	Understand; believe
___ 20. taunted	H.	The state or act of looking forward to something
___ 21. rancid	I.	Elaborately
___ 22. ornately	J.	Enthusiasm

Vocabulary - *When the Legends Die* Chapters 22-32

Part I: Using Prior Knowledge and Contextual Clues

    Below are the sentences in which the vocabulary words appear in the text. Read the sentence. Use any clues you can find in the sentence combined with your prior knowledge, and write what you think the underlined words mean on the lines provided.

23. "Odds?" Red laughed derisively, "The boy just got thrown and you want me to give odds!

_____

24. He held to the saddle until he had his equilibrium, then took off his bedroll

_____

25. Meo was his taciturn self again, saying little, keeping his thoughts to himself.

_____

26. And, with Red Dillon, a world of noisy saloons, smoky pool halls, ratty little hotels, fly-specked chili parlors, conniving bettors.

_____

27. He saw the hard, calculating look in her eyes, the provocative smile on her lips.

_____

28. Red reached in his pocket, found nothing there, glanced at Tom, then sat disconsolate.

_____

29. Veteran riders and ropers went to Odessa to test their skills and reflexes and weigh them against the inevitability of time.

_____

30. There were the events that meant nothing to him, the bull riding, the calf roping, the steer wrestling, the trick riding, sometimes the inconsequentials of a horse show.

_____

Legends Vocabulary Chapters 22-32 Continued

Part II: Determining the Meaning - Match the vocabulary words to their dictionary definitions.

___ 23. derisively
___ 24. equilibrium
___ 25. taciturn
___ 26. conniving
___ 27. provocative
___ 28. disconsolate
___ 29. inevitability
___ 30. inconsequentials

A. Untalkative
B. Gloomy; hopelessly sad
C. In a scoffing or ridiculing manner
D. Quality of not being able to be avoided
E. Balance
F. Things that don't matter or don't have any significance
G. Tending to provoke; exciting; stimulating
H. Conspiring; pretending ignorance of a wrong

Vocabulary - *When the Legends Die* Chapters 33-41

Part I: Using Prior Knowledge and Contextual Clues
    Below are the sentences in which the vocabulary words appear in the text. Read the sentence. Use any clues you can find in the sentence combined with your prior knowledge, and write what you think the underlined words mean on the lines provided.

31. The valley was gray with <u>acrid</u> smoke, held close by the night's damp air

_____

32. . . . goading the horse to violent, <u>malevolent</u> action.

_____

33. They sat silent when he rode because they were awed and <u>morbidly</u> fascinated.

_____

34. The comment was <u>ambiguous</u>, and intended so

_____

35. She straightened his bed, <u>deft</u> and efficient

_____

36. She was the most skillful of the nurses, the most <u>solicitous</u> and helpful, the most friendly.

_____

Part II: Determining the Meaning - Match the vocabulary words to their dictionary definitions.

   ___ 31. acrid   A. Harsh to the taste or smell
   ___ 32. malevolent   B. Indefinite; open to several interpretations
   ___ 33. morbidly   C. Attentive; full of desire; eager
   ___ 34. ambiguous   D. Skillful
   ___ 35. deft   E. In a manner preoccupied by unwholesome matters
   ___ 36. solicitous   F. Malicious; evil; wishing harm to others

Vocabulary - *When the Legends Die* Chapters 42-49

Part I: Using Prior Knowledge and Contextual Clues
　　Use any clues you can find in the sentence combined with your prior knowledge, and write what you think the underlined words mean on the lines provided.

37. He ordered the dogs to go pull the flock together, but they were <u>baffled</u> by his words.

_____

38. It would take a few days to get <u>acclimated</u> again.

_____

39. . . . its chances of survival this long were slim, with <u>persistent</u> hunters and bear-hating ranchmen.

_____

40. He laughed at that, a snorting laugh of <u>derision</u>.

_____

41. He said it defiantly, then was silent, <u>abashed</u> and somehow sorry he had said it.

_____

42. He waited, staring at the dark, shadowy mound of the <u>cache</u>.

_____

43. If he had missed the heart with the first shot the bear, numbed to further pain, would have taken a whole magazine of bullets and kept coming, an <u>infuriated</u> devil.

_____

44. He sewed to the end of the sinew and drew another strand from his mouth, remembering the <u>penance</u> trip up the mountain.

Part II: Determining the Meaning - Match the vocabulary words to their dictionary definitions.

___ 37. baffled　　　　　A. Ashamed; embarrassed
___ 38. acclimated　　　B. A hole where things can be hidden
___ 39. persistent　　　C. An act done to show repentance for a wrongdoing
___ 40. derision　　　　D. Refusing to give up or let go
___ 41. abashed　　　　 E. Puzzled; perplexed; confused
___ 42. cache　　　　　 F. Became used to a condition
___ 43. infuriated　　　G. Ridicule; scoffing; mocking
___ 44. penance　　　　 H. Made very angry

ANSWER KEY - VOCABULARY
When the Legends Die

Chapters 1-7	Chapters 8-12	Chapters 13-21	Chapters 22-32
1. D	7. B	13. H	23. C
2. A	8. D	14. D	24. E
3. F	9. A	15. C	25. A
4. B	10. F	16. G	26. H
5. C	11. C	17. J	27. G
6. E	12. E	18. A	28. B
		19. E	29. D
		20. B	30. F
		21. F	
		22. I	

Chapters 33-41	Chapters 42-49
31. A	37. E
32. F	38. F
33. E	39. D
34. B	40. G
35. D	41. A
36. C	42. B
	43. H
	44. C

DAILY LESSONS

LESSON ONE

Objectives
1. To introduce the *When the Legends Die* unit.
2. To distribute books and other related materials (study guides, reading assignments, project assignment etc.).
3. To preview the study questions for chapters 1-7
4. To familiarize students with the vocabulary for chapters 1-7
5. To read chapters 1-7
6. To give students the opportunity to practice writing their own personal opinions
7. To give the teacher the opportunity to evaluate students' writing skills

Activity #1

Distribute Writing Assignment #1. Discuss the directions in detail and give students ample time to complete the assignment.

Transition: Ask students to give some of their ideas as to what the quotation means. Tell students that the quotation came from the book they are about to read, *When the Legends Die*. Explain that you'll talk more about this quotation later, after they have read the book, to see if after reading the book the quotation has any different meaning for them.

Activity #2

Distribute the materials students will use in this unit. Explain in detail how students are to use these materials.

Study Guides Students should read the study guide questions for each reading assignment prior to beginning the reading assignment to get a feeling for what events and ideas are important in the section they are about to read. After reading the section, students will (as a class or individually) answer the questions to review the important events and ideas from that section of the book. Students should keep the study guides as study materials for the unit test.

Vocabulary Prior to reading a reading assignment, students will do vocabulary work related to the section of the book they are about to read. Following the completion of the reading of the book, there will be a vocabulary review of all the words used in the vocabulary assignments. Students should keep their vocabulary work as study materials for the unit test.

Reading Assignment Sheet You need to fill in the reading assignment sheet to let students know by when their reading has to be completed. You can either write the assignment sheet up on a side blackboard or bulletin board and leave it there for students to see each day, or you can "ditto" copies for each student to have. In either case, you should advise students to become very familiar with the reading assignments so they know what is expected of them.

Extra Activities Center   The Unit Resource portion of this unit contains suggestions for an extra library of related books and articles in your classroom as well as crossword and word search puzzles. Make an extra activities center in your room where you will keep these materials for students to use. (Bring the books and articles in from the library and keep several copies of the puzzles on hand.) Explain to students that these materials are available for students to use when they finish reading assignments or other class work early.

Nonfiction Assignment Sheet   Explain to students that they each are to read at least one non-fiction piece from the in-class library at some time during the unit. Students will fill out a nonfiction assignment sheet after completing the reading to help you evaluate their reading experiences and to help the students think about and evaluate their own reading experiences.

Books   Each school has its own rules and regulations regarding student use of school books. Advise students of the procedures that are normal for your school.

Activity #3

Preview the study questions and show students how to do the vocabulary work for Chapters 1-7 of *When the Legends Die*. Tell students that they should have this work completed prior to your next class meeting.

WRITING ASSIGNMENT #1 - *When the Legends Die*

PROMPT
Your assignment is to write a composition in which you explain what you think this statement means:

"When the legends die, the dreams end.
 When the dreams end, there is no more greatness."

PREWRITING
The first thing you need to do is to stop and think about the quotation. Jot down your responses to the following questions: What are legends? What are dreams? What is greatness? What does the quotation mean? Why do you think it means that? (Jot down two or three things that lead you to believe that is what the quotation means.)

DRAFTING
There is no special format for this assignment. Just write a few paragraphs telling what you think the quotation means and why you think it means that.

PROMPT
When you finish the rough draft of your composition, ask a student who sits near you to read it. After reading your rough draft, he/she should tell you what he/she liked best about your work, which parts were difficult to understand, and ways in which your work could be improved. Reread your paper considering your critic's comments, and make the corrections you think are necessary.

PROOFREADING
Do a final proofreading of your composition double-checking your grammar, spelling, organization, and the clarity of your ideas.

NONFICTION ASSIGNMENT SHEET
(To be completed after reading the required nonfiction article)

Name _____ Date _____

Title of Nonfiction Read _____

Written By _____ Publication Date _____

I. Factual Summary: Write a short summary of the piece you read.

II. Vocabulary
    1. With which vocabulary words in the piece did you encounter some degree of difficulty?

    2. How did you resolve your lack of understanding with these words?

III. Interpretation: What was the main point the author wanted you to get from reading his work?

IV. Criticism
    1. With which points of the piece did you agree or find easy to accept? Why?

    2. With which points of the piece did you disagree or find difficult to believe? Why?

V. Personal Response: What do you think about this piece? <u>OR</u> How does this piece influence your ideas?

LESSON TWO

Objectives
1. To read chapters 1-7
2. To give students practice reading orally
3. To evaluate students' oral reading

Activity

Have students read chapters 1-7 of *When the Legends Die* out loud in class. You probably know the best way to get readers with your class; pick students at random, ask for volunteers, or use whatever method works best for your group. If you have not yet completed an oral reading evaluation for your students this marking period, this would be a good opportunity to do so. A form is included with this unit for your convenience.

If students do not complete reading chapters 1-7 in class, they should do so prior to your next class meeting.

LESSON THREE

Objectives
1. To review the main events and ideas from chapters 1-7
2. To preview the study questions for chapters 8-12
3. To familiarize students with the vocabulary in chapters 8-12
4. To read chapters 8-12

Activity #1

Give students a few minutes to formulate answers for the study guide questions for chapters 1-7, and then discuss the answers to the questions in detail. Write the answers on the board or overhead transparency so students can have the correct answers for study purposes. Note: It is a good practice in public speaking and leadership skills for individual students to take charge of leading the discussions of the study questions. Perhaps a different student could go to the front of the class and lead the discussion each day that the study questions are discussed during this unit. Of course, the teacher should guide the discussion when appropriate and be sure to fill in any gaps the students leave.

Activity #2

Give students about fifteen minutes to preview the study questions for
chapters 8-12 of *When the Legends Die* and to do the related vocabulary work.

Activity #3

Have students read chapters 8-12 of *When the Legends Die* orally in class. Continue the oral reading evaluations. If students do not complete reading chapters 8-12 in class, they should do so prior to your next class meeting.

ORAL READING EVALUATION - *When the Legends Die*

Name _____ Class____ Date _____

SKILL	EXCELLENT	GOOD	AVERAGE	FAIR	POOR
Fluency	5	4	3	2	1
Clarity	5	4	3	2	1
Audibility	5	4	3	2	1
Pronunciation	5	4	3	2	1
_____	5	4	3	2	1
_____	5	4	3	2	1

Total _____   Grade _____

Comments:

LESSONS FOUR AND FIVE

Objectives
1. To review the main ideas and events from chapters 8-12
2. To introduce the research project
3. To preview and read chapters 13-21

Activity #1
Give students a few minutes to formulate answers to the study questions for chapters 8-12. Discuss students' answers in detail. Write the correct answers on the board for students to copy for study use later.

Activity #2
Tell students that prior to your next class period they should do the prereading work (previewing study questions and doing prereading vocabulary worksheet) for chapters 13-21.

Activity #3
Explain to students that they are each to find and read about two different legends and be prepared to tell the class about it by Lesson Nine. (Give students a day/date.) The legends can be from American Folklore, Indian legends, local legends, or legends from any culture in the world.

Activity #4
Take your students to the library to do their research. You might review the places where they would be likely to find the information they need. After students find a legend, they should use their remaining class time to read about it.

LESSON SIX

Objectives
1. To review the main events and ideas from chapters 13-21
2. To preview the study questions for chapters 22-32
3. To familiarize students with the vocabulary in chapters 22-32
4. To read chapters 22-32
5. To give students the opportunity to work on their legends research projects

Activity #1
Give students a few minutes to formulate answers for the study guide questions for chapters 13-21, and then discuss the answers to the questions in detail. Write the answers on the board or overhead transparency so students can have the correct answers for study purposes.

Activity #2
Tell students that prior to your next class meeting they should have completed the prereading and reading work for chapters 22-32. Students may use the remainder of this class period to work on this assignment or to work on their legends research project.

LESSON SEVEN

Objectives
1. To review the main events and ideas from chapters 22-32
2. To preview the study questions for chapters 33-41
3. To familiarize students with the vocabulary in chapters 33-41
4. To read chapters 33-41

Activity #1
Give students a few minutes to formulate answers for the study guide questions for chapters 22-32, and then discuss the answers to the questions in detail. Write the answers on the board or overhead transparency so students can have the correct answers for study purposes.

Activity #2
Give students the remainder of the class period to do the prereading work for chapters 33-41 and to read those chapters silently.

LESSON EIGHT

Objectives
    1. To give students the opportunity to practice writing to inform
    2. To help students prepare for their group presentations
    3. To give the teacher the opportunity to evaluate students' writing skills
    4. To review the main events and ideas from chapters 33-41
    5. To do the prereading and reading work for chapters 42-49

Activity #1
    Give students a few minutes to formulate answers for the study questions for chapters 33-41 (Or, if you prefer, give students a quiz on chapters 33-41 to make sure they have done the assigned reading.) Discuss the answers to the study questions in detail.

Activity #2
    Tell students that prior to your next class period they should have done the prereading and reading work for chapters 42-49.

Activity #3
    Distribute Writing Assignment #2. Discuss the directions in detail and give students ample time to complete the assignment.

LESSONS NINE AND TEN

Objectives
    1. To broaden students' knowledge of legends
    2. To review the main ideas and events of chapters 42-49
    3. To give students practice public speaking
    4. To bring the research project to a close

Activity #1
    Give students a few minutes to formulate answers to the study questions for chapters 42-49. Discuss the answers in detail.

Activity #2
    Begin the oral presentations. The number of class periods devoted to the reports depends on the length of your class period and the abilities of your students. This unit schedules one and a half class periods. If you need more, just insert an extra day.

WRITING ASSIGNMENT #2 - *When the Legends Die*

PROMPT

You have researched at least one legend. You have done the research and will soon have to give a presentation to the class. As part of the evaluation of your work, and to help you prepare your oral presentation, your assignment is to write a composition in which you explain the legend you researched.

PREWRITING

Gather together the notes you took as you were researching your legend. Organize them into a logical fashion, making a little outline of your main ideas.

DRAFTING

Write a paragraph in which you introduce the legend you researched. Tell what kind of a legend it is and where it is from.

Write a paragraph or two telling the story of the legend.

Write a concluding paragraph in which you give your own thoughts about the legend..

PROMPT

When you finish the rough draft of your paper, ask a student who sits near you to read it. After reading your rough draft, he/she should tell you what he/she liked best about your work, which parts were difficult to understand, and ways in which your work could be improved. Reread your paper considering your critic's comments, and make the corrections you think are necessary.

PROOFREADING

Do a final proofreading of your paper double-checking your grammar, spelling, organization, and the clarity of your ideas.

LESSON TEN

Objective

To discuss *When the Legends Die* on interpretive and critical levels

Activity

Choose the questions from the Extra Discussion Questions/Writing Assignments which seem most appropriate for your students. A class discussion of these questions is most effective if students have been given the opportunity to formulate answers to the questions prior to the discussion. To this end, you may either have all the students formulate answers to all the questions, divide your class into groups and assign one or more questions to each group, or you could assign one question to each student in your class. The option you choose will make a difference in the amount of class time needed for this activity.

Activity #3

After students have had ample time to formulate answers to the questions, begin your class discussion of the questions and the ideas presented by the questions. Be sure students take notes during the discussion so they have information to study for the unit test.

EXTRA WRITING ASSIGNMENTS/DISCUSSION QUESTIONS - *When the Legends Die*

<u>Interpretation</u>

1. What are the main conflicts in the story and how are they resolved?

2. In what way is the setting important to the story?

3. From what point(s) of view is the story written.?

4. Where is the climax of the story? Justify your answer.

5. Which events in the novel are "turning points"--events which affect the course of the plot?

6. Is there any humor in the story? If so, where. If not, why not?

7. All along, people kept "helping" Thomas. How did Blue Elk, Benny Grayback, and Red Dillon claim to be trying to help him, and what in fact were the end results of their efforts?

8. Who were Thomas' true friends? Explain your choices.

<u>Critical</u>

9. Explain the significance of the title of the book

10. Is the story of *When the Legends Die* believable? Why or why not?

11. Do any of the characters change in the course of the novel? If so, who and how?

12. Are the characters in *When the Legends Die* stereotypes? Explain your answer.

13. Compare and contrast Thomas with Blue Elk.

14. Compare and contrast Blue Elk and Red Dillon.

15. What was the purpose of the appearance of the All-Mother?

16. Compare and contrast Thomas and his father, George.

17. Explain the importance of rhythm in *When the Legends Die*.

18. Was education important to Thomas? Why or why not? What kinds of education were shown in this book?

When the Legends Die Extra Discussion Questions Page 2

19. Discuss the role of money in *When the Legends Die*.

20. Why was Meo included in the story?

21. What were the "songs"? What was their purpose?

22. Compare and contrast Dolly Beaverfoot and Rowena Ellis.

23. Explore the role of death in the story. Compare and contrast the deaths of George, Bessie, Red Dillon, Meo, and the animals.

24. Compare Thomas' life to the breaking of a bronco.

25. Characterize Hal Borland's style of writing. How does it contribute to the value of the novel?

26. Explain how Thomas Black Bull's name changed during different phases of his life, and explain how those changes were appropriate.

27. Explain the meaning of this quotation in relation to the story: "When the legends die, the dreams end. When the dreams end, there is no more greatness."

Personal Response

28. What does it mean to trust someone? How do you feel when you trust someone and that person betrays your trust. Explore the role of trust and betrayed trust in this novel.

29. How might the story have changed if Thomas had not been baptized?

30. Would you have liked to have been a part of life in this book? Why or why not?

31. If you could be any of the characters in the book for a short time, which one would you choose? Why?

32. Did you enjoy reading *When the Legends Die*? Why or why not?

LESSON TWELVE

Objective
    To review all of the vocabulary work done in this unit

Activity
    Choose one (or more) of the vocabulary review activities listed below and spend your class period as directed in the activity. Some of the materials for these review activities are located in the Vocabulary Resource section of this unit.

VOCABULARY REVIEW ACTIVITIES

1. Divide your class into two teams and have an old-fashioned spelling or definition bee.

2. Give each of your students (or students in groups of two, three or four) a *When the Legends Die* Vocabulary Word Search Puzzle. The person (group) to find all of the vocabulary words in the puzzle first wins.

3. Give students a *When the Legends Die* Vocabulary Word Search Puzzle without the word list. The person or group to find the most vocabulary words in the puzzle wins.

4. Use a *When the Legends Die* Vocabulary Crossword Puzzle. Put the puzzle onto a transparency on the overhead projector (so everyone can see it), and do the puzzle together as a class.

5. Give students a *When the Legends Die* Vocabulary Matching Worksheet to do.

6. Divide your class into two teams. Use the *When the Legends Die* vocabulary words with their letters jumbled as a word list. Student 1 from Team A faces off against Student 1 from Team B. You write the first jumbled word on the board. The first student (1A or 1B) to unscramble the word wins the chance for his/her team to score points. If 1A wins the jumble, go to student 2A and give him/her a definition. He/she must give you the correct spelling of the vocabulary word which fits that definition. If he/she does, Team A scores a point, and you give student 3A a definition for which you expect a correctly spelled matching vocabulary word. Continue giving Team A definitions until some team member makes an incorrect response. An incorrect response sends the game back to the jumbled-word face off, this time with students 2A and 2B. Instead of repeating giving definitions to the first few students of each team, continue with the student after the one who gave the last incorrect response on the team. For example, if Team B wins the jumbled-word face-off, and student 5B gave the last incorrect answer for Team B, you would start this round of definition questions with student 6B, and so on. The team with the most points wins!

7. Have students write a story in which they correctly use as many vocabulary words as possible. Have students read their compositions orally! Post the most original compositions on your bulletin board!

LESSON THIRTEEN

Objectives
1. To give students the opportunity to practice writing to persuade
2. To give the teacher the opportunity to evaluate students' writing skills

Activity #1
Take your students to the library/media center so they have research materials readily at hand. Distribute Writing Assignment #3. Discuss the directions in detail and give students ample time to complete the assignment.

It would probably be very helpful to students if you would have a little brainstorming session with them to help them think of issues relating to the environment about which they could write.

Activity #2
While students are doing their group work, call individual students to your desk or some other private area where you can hold a writing conference to discuss students' first writing assignments. A Writing Evaluation Form is included for your convenience.

LESSON FOURTEEN

Objectives
1. To review the basics of sentence structure
2. To give students the opportunity to experiment with sentence structure
3. To show students that the same essential thoughts can be expressed in different ways, but also that by changing sentence structure one sometimes also slightly changes the meaning of the sentence

Activity #1
Take the first part of the class period to review the basics of sentence structure: simple sentences, compound sentences, complex sentences, and compound-complex sentences.

Activity #2
Distribute the Sentence Structure Worksheet, discuss the directions in detail, give students ample time to complete the worksheet. Depending on the level of your class, you may want to do Part One together as a class to show students what you expect of them when they do Part Two on their own.

When the students finish the worksheet, discuss their answers in detail.

WRITING ASSIGNMENT #3 - *When the Legends Die*

PROMPT

Hal Borland, author of *When the Legends Die* won many awards for his writing about nature. He clearly had a respect and a love for nature, which many people today do not seem to have. Your assignment is to choose an issue relating to the environment, research a little bit about it, and write a letter to your government official (mayor, governor, representative, senator, etc.) persuading him/her to your viewpoint on that issue.

PREWRITING

This assignment gives you a lot of leeway to find an issue that interests you, whether it would be related to toxic dumping, trash in your local park, air pollution, or any of hundreds of other topics related to the environment.

Decide on a topic that is of interest to you. Do a little research: read at least two or three articles about that topic before you sit down to write your letter. (Don't forget to fill out a Nonfiction Reading Assignment Sheet for the nonfiction research articles you read.)

Decide to whom it would be best to address your letter and find that person's mailing address.

Outline your thoughts so you can present them in a logical order in your letter.

DRAFTING

Use a business letter format.

Write an introductory paragraph in which you introduce yourself and the issue about which you wish to voice an opinion. State your main point and then use the rest of your letter to convince your reader to agree with you. Use facts you found in your research to help add credibility to your arguments.

PROMPT

After you have completed your writing, give your letter to a friend to read. After reading your rough draft, he/she should tell you what he/she liked best about your work, which parts were difficult to understand, and ways in which your work could be improved. Reread your paper considering your critic's comments, and make the corrections you think are necessary.

PROOFREADING

Do a final proofreading of your paper double-checking your grammar, spelling, organization, and the clarity of your ideas.

SENTENCE STRUCTURE WORKSHEET - *When the Legends Die*

Part One: Look at each of the sentences in the following paragraph from *When the Legends Die*. Determine the sentence type for each sentence then offer suggestions as to ways the sentence(s) could be rewritten in different sentence types.

"He came to the spring that evening. It was dusk, but she saw him. He stepped out of the deep shadows and took the three willow twigs from the moss, and then he was gone. She said her thanks to the earth and sky and the quarters of the earth, and when she had done that she drew the blankets around herself and the boy and they slept. He knew they had come."

Part Two: Determine the sentence type for each sentence then offer suggestions as to ways the sentence(s) could be rewritten in different sentence types.

"He did not remember that song. He said that a rifle was better than a song for killing deer, but he didn't dare use the rifle yet. `People did not starve before they had rifles,' she said. And that night she taught him the song for hunting deer. The next afternoon when the sun was near setting they sang the song. Then he took his bow and the arrows and went to the pool, and that night he killed a fat doe with the arrows. He said it was good to know that song, and he made a small bow and blunt bird arrows and taught the boy to use them.

"She made meat. She made leather. She made bags to store the meat and she made leggings and shirts for the man and the boy. She remembered the things her mother had taught her and it was like the old days.

WRITING EVALUATION FORM - *When the Legends Die*

Name _____ Date _____

Grade _____

Circle One For Each Item:

Grammar: excellent   good   fair   poor

Spelling: excellent   good   fair   poor

Punctuation: excellent   good   fair   poor

Legibility: excellent   good   fair   poor

Strengths:

Weaknesses:

Comments/Suggestions:

LESSON SIXTEEN

Objective
    To review the main ideas presented in *When the Legends Die*

Activity #1
    Choose one of the review games/activities included in this unit and spend your class period as outlined there. Some materials for these activities are located in the Unit Resource section of this unit.

Activity #2
    Remind students that the Unit Test will be in the next class meeting. Stress the review of the Study Guides and their class notes as a last minute, brush-up review for homework.

REVIEW GAMES/ACTIVITIES - *When the Legends Die*

1. Ask the class to make up a unit test for *When the Legends Die*. The test should have 4 sections: matching, true/false, short answer, and essay. Students may use 1/2 period to make the test and then swap papers and use the other 1/2 class period to take a test a classmate has devised. (open book) You may want to use the unit test included in this unit or take questions from the students' unit tests to formulate your own test.

2. Take 1/2 period for students to make up true and false questions (including the answers). Collect the papers and divide the class into two teams. Draw a big tic-tac-toe board on the chalk board. Make one team X and one team O. Ask questions to each side, giving each student one turn. If the question is answered correctly, that students' team's letter (X or O) is placed in the box. If the answer is incorrect, no mark is placed in the box. The object is to get three marks in a row like tic-tac-toe. You may want to keep track of the number of games won for each team.

3. Take 1/2 period for students to make up questions (true/false and short answer). Collect the questions. Divide the class into two teams. You'll alternate asking questions to individual members of teams A & B (like in a spelling bee). The question keeps going from A to B until it is correctly answered, then a new question is asked. A correct answer does not allow the team to get another question. Correct answers are +2 points; incorrect answers are -1 point.

4. Have students pair up and quiz each other from their study guides and class notes.

5. Give students a *When the Legends Die* crossword puzzle to complete.

6. Divide your class into two teams. Use the *When the Legends Die* crossword words with their letters jumbled as a word list. Student 1 from Team A faces off against Student 1 from Team B. You write the first jumbled word on the board. The first student (1A or 1B) to unscramble the word wins the chance for his/her team to score points. If 1A wins the jumble, go to student 2A and give him/her a clue. He/she must give you the correct word which matches that clue. If he/she does, Team A scores a point, and you give student 3A a clue for which you expect another correct response. Continue giving Team A clues until some team member makes an incorrect response. An incorrect response sends the game back to the jumbled-word face off, this time with students 2A and 2B. Instead of repeating giving clues to the first few students of each team, continue with the student after the one who gave the last incorrect response on the team. For example, if Team B wins the jumbled-word face-off, and student 5B gave the last incorrect answer for Team B, you would start this round of clue questions with student 6B, and so on. The team with the most points wins!

UNIT TESTS

SHORT ANSWER UNIT TEST 1 - *When the Legends Die*

I. Matching

___ 1. Bessie   A. Thomas' roommate

___ 2. Jim Thatcher   B. Author

___ 3. Benny Grayback   C. Nurse

___ 4. George   D. English teacher

___ 5. Hal Borland   E. Tended his beans and peppers

___ 6. Red Dillon   F. Killer Tom; Bear's Brother

___ 7. Thomas Black Bull   G. Carpentry teacher

___ 8. Rowena Ellis   H. Burned Thomas' lodge

___ 9. Luther   I. Killed Frank No Deer

___ 10. Meo   J. Owned a sheep ranch

___ 11. Neil Swanson   K. Store owner

___ 12. Albert Left Hand   L. Bet on Tom at the rodeos

___ 13. Mary Redmond   M. Bear's Brother's Mother

___ 14. Blue Elk   N. Flogged Thomas for fighting

When the Legends Die Short Answer Unit Test 1 Page 2

II. Short Answer

1. Why did George and his family go to the mountains?

2. What was the problem about working at the sawmill and having credit at the store?

3. What is the "roundness"?

4. How did the boy come to have a bear cub as a pet?

5. Describe how Thomas' bear was returned to the wild.

6. Why did Thomas return to the school of his own free will after he escaped?

When the Legends Die Short Answer Unit Test 1 Page 3

7. How did Thomas learn to ride wild colts?

8. What was Red's scam?

9. Describe Tom's riding style after Red's death.

10. Why wouldn't Tom go to Nyack?

11. What job did Tom take to earn some money while his body finished healing?

12. Why did Tom go back to Horse Mountain to look for the bear?

13. Why didn't Tom kill the bear?

When the Legends Die Short Answer Unit Test 1 Page 4

III. Essay

Pretend you are Thomas Black Bull. Based on your experiences in life, write a letter to your son or daughter giving him or her advice about life. If you were Thomas Black Bull, what advice would you give to your children? Explain why.

IV. Vocabulary

Listen to the vocabulary words and write them down. Go back later and write in the correct definitions next to the words.

1.

2.

3.

4.

5.

6.

7.

8.

9.

10.

KEY: SHORT ANSWER UNIT TEST #1 - *When the Legends Die*

I. Matching/Identify

M	1. Bessie	A.	Thomas' roommate
K	2. Jim Thatcher	B.	Author
G	3. Benny Grayback	C.	Nurse
I	4. George	D.	English teacher
B	5. Hal Borland	E.	Tended his beans and peppers
L	6. Red Dillon	F.	Killer Tom; Bear's Brother
F	7. Thomas Black Bull	G.	Carpentry teacher
D	8. Rowena Ellis	H.	Burned Thomas' lodge
A	9. Luther	I.	Killed Frank No Deer
E	10. Meo	J.	Owned a sheep ranch
N	11. Neil Swanson	K.	Store owner
J	12. Albert Left Hand	L.	Bet on Tom at the rodeos
C	13. Mary Redmond	M.	Bear's Brother's Mother
H	14. Blue Elk	N.	Flogged Thomas for fighting

II. Short Answer

1. Why did George and his family go to the mountains?
George killed Frank No Deer. He and his family fled to the mountains to get away from trouble.

2. What was the problem about working at the sawmill and having credit at the store?
The Indians could never quite make enough to pay off their store debts, and they could not quit working as long as they had a debt at the store. Without careful planning, a person would have to work indefinitely at the sawmill.

3. What is the "roundness"?
The roundness describes the natural way of life; things in nature are round, as opposed to the things of man which are angular.

4. How did the boy come to have a bear cub as a pet?
A stranger came and killed the she-bear and one of her cubs, leaving the other cub. The boy befriended the cub of his bear friend, and the cub responded.

5. Describe how Thomas' bear was returned to the wild.
Blue Elk took Thomas and the bear to Horse Mountain. He chained the bear to a tree and told Thomas that he would leave the bear there to die unless Thomas would agree to send the bear home and to return to the school himself.

6. Why did Thomas return to the school of his own free will after he escaped?
When he returned to his lodge home, he found it was burned to the ground. He had lost his home and his friend. There was nothing left in the wild for him. He decided the old ways must be dead, so he returned to the school.

7. How did Thomas learn to ride wild colts?
Since he was a terrible farmer, the administrators at the school sent him out to tend to the wild horses. He wondered what it would be like to ride a wild horse, tried it, and eventually learned a way to master the animals.

8. What was Red's scam?
He rode into town with Thomas, making people believe that Thomas was a kid who thought he could ride. He'd place small bets on Thomas in the early rounds, which Thomas would usually win, then he'd tell Thomas to lose in the finals. By losing the bets in the finals, he could then talk people into setting up a special event. Then, he would place large bets, and he would order Thomas to ride his best to win. In this way, he would collect large sums of money from the event.

9. Describe Tom's riding style after Red's death.

   He started riding to punish the horse, to bring out the worst the horse could give, instead of riding clean for points. He didn't care whether he won or not; his ride was for the battle between himself and the horse.

10. Why wouldn't Tom go to Nyack?

    Tom thought Mary was trying to run his life like Red, Blue Elk, and the others had done. He wanted to be independent.

11. What job did Tom take to earn some money while his body finished healing?

    He became a sheep herder.

12. Why did Tom go back to Horse Mountain to look for the bear?

    The bear was the one last remaining thing from his past to remind him he was an Indian. He wanted to kill the bear and make a clean break from his past.

13. Why didn't Tom kill the bear?

    His ancestral ties with nature deep within him would not let him kill the bear just for the sake of killing. The bear had done nothing to harm him. To have killed the bear would have been to completely go against all of his instincts and the beliefs he had held for so long. He could not make a total break with the past.

III. Essay: Answers will vary.

IV. Vocabulary

   Choose ten of the vocabulary words to read orally for students to write down.

SHORT ANSWER UNIT TEST 2 - *When the Legends Die*

I. Matching

___ 1. Bessie   A. Store owner

___ 2. Jim Thatcher   B. Bet on Tom at the rodeos

___ 3. Benny Grayback   C. Bear's Brother's Mother

___ 4. George   D. Flogged Thomas for fighting

___ 5. Hal Borland   E. Killed Frank No Deer

___ 6. Red Dillon   F. Burned Thomas' lodge

___ 7. Thomas Black Bull   G. Owned a sheep ranch

___ 8. Rowena Ellis   H. Killer Tom; Bear's Brother

___ 9. Luther   I. Tended his beans and peppers

___ 10. Meo   J. Carpentry teacher

___ 11. Neil Swanson   K. Thomas' roommate

___ 12. Albert Left Hand   L. Author

___ 13. Mary Redmond   M. Nurse

___ 14. Blue Elk   N. English teacher

When the Legends Die Short Answer Unit Test 2 Page 2

II. Short Answer

1. What was the problem about working at the sawmill and having credit at the store?

2. Why did George kill Frank No Deer?

3. How did George die?

4. Why did Blue Elk go into the woods to find the boy?

5. What did Thomas think of plowing?

6. Why did Tom have a losing streak?

When the Legends Die Short Answer Unit Test 2 Page 3

7. Describe Tom's attitude towards life after Meo died.

8. Describe Tom's ride on Sky Rocket and the results.

9. Why did Tom go back to Horse Mountain to look for the bear?

10. What was the All-Mother?

11. What did Tom say to the deer picture?

12. How did Tom change at the end of the story?

When the Legends Die Short Answer Unit Test 2 Page 4

III. Composition

1. What were the "songs" in the story, and what was their purpose?

2. What was the main conflict in the story. Defend your choice.

When the Legends Die Short Answer Unit Test 2 Page 5

IV. Vocabulary

Listen to the vocabulary word and spell it. After you have spelled all the words, go back and write down the definitions.

1.

2.

3.

4.

5.

6.

7.

8.

9.

10.

KEY: SHORT ANSWER UNIT TEST 2 *When the Legends Die*

I. Matching (Use this matching key also for the Advanced Short Answer Unit Test)

_C_	1. Bessie	A.	Store owner
_A_	2. Jim Thatcher	B.	Bet on Tom at the rodeos
_J_	3. Benny Grayback	C.	Bear's Brother's Mother
_E_	4. George	D.	Flogged Thomas for fighting
_L_	5. Hal Borland	E.	Killed Frank No Deer
_B_	6. Red Dillon	F.	Burned Thomas' lodge
_H_	7. Thomas Black Bull	G.	Owned a sheep ranch
_N_	8. Rowena Ellis	H.	Killer Tom; Bear's Brother
_K_	9. Luther	I.	Tended his beans and peppers
_I_	10. Meo	J.	Carpentry teacher
_D_	11. Neil Swanson	K.	Thomas' roommate
_G_	12. Albert Left Hand	L.	Author
_M_	13. Mary Redmond	M.	Nurse
_F_	14. Blue Elk	N.	English teacher

II. Short Answer

1. What was the problem about working at the sawmill and having credit at the store?
   The Indians could never quite make enough to pay off their store debts, and they could not quit working as long as they had a debt at the store. Without careful planning, a person would have to work indefinitely at the sawmill.

2. Why did George kill Frank No Deer?
   George had been working to save enough money to pay off the store debt so he would be free to leave the sawmill. Each time he had saved up a substantial amount of money, Frank No Deer stole the money. George killed him for stealing his money.

3. How did George die?
   He was killed in an avalanche while out hunting for meat.

4. Why did Blue Elk go into the woods to find the boy?
   The preacher hired him to do it. Because the preacher had baptized the boy, he felt a responsibility towards the boy since his parents were dead, so he sent Blue Elk to get the boy and take him to school.

5. What did Thomas think of plowing?
   He thought it was senseless to try to make the land grow something that wasn't there naturally. He thought the land would do better left to its own ways, and that walking up and down rows was a waste of time since you didn't go anywhere with your walking.

6. Why did Tom have a losing streak?
   He started riding for the crowd instead of concentrating on the ride itself.

7. Describe Tom's attitude towards life after Meo died.
   Tom outwardly appeared to be mad at the world. He didn't care about anything except those few moments when he was riding.

8. Describe Tom's ride on Sky Rocket and the results.
   Tom tried to muscle Sky Rocket, and his leg went numb. In order to hold on, he dug his spurs into the horse's side, making the animal even more vicious. Tom jerked the animal's head, pulling the animal off balance. The animal fell, crushing Tom on the ground. He had a punctured lung, a concussion, a broken pelvis, and a broken femur.

9. Why did Tom go back to Horse Mountain to look for the bear?
   The bear was the one last remaining thing from his past to remind him he was an Indian. He wanted to kill the bear and make a clean break from his past.

10. What was the All-Mother?
    The All-Mother was a vision Tom had, a woman who represented all of the mothers and grandmothers back to the beginning of time.

11. What did Tom say to the deer picture?
    He apologized for killing her sister and wasting the meat. He promised to make use of every part of the next deer he would kill.

12. How did Tom change at the end of the story?
    He began to live his life in the old way once more, realizing that he could not hide from his roots, he could not change who he was. Instead of fighting to put the past away, he faced it and accepted it as a part of his life.

III. Composition: Answers will vary.

IV. Vocabulary
    Choose ten of the vocabulary words to dictate to your students for this section of the test.

ADVANCED SHORT ANSWER UNIT TEST - *When the Legends Die*

I. Matching

___ 1. Bessie   A. Store owner

___ 2. Jim Thatcher   B. Bet on Tom at the rodeos

___ 3. Benny Grayback   C. Bear's Brother's Mother

___ 4. George   D. Flogged Thomas for fighting

___ 5. Hal Borland   E. Killed Frank No Deer

___ 6. Red Dillon   F. Burned Thomas' lodge

___ 7. Thomas Black Bull   G. Owned a sheep ranch

___ 8. Rowena Ellis   H. Killer Tom; Bear's Brother

___ 9. Luther   I. Tended his beans and peppers

___ 10. Meo   J. Carpentry teacher

___ 11. Neil Swanson   K. Thomas' roommate

___ 12. Albert Left Hand   L. Author

___ 13. Mary Redmond   M. Nurse

___ 14. Blue Elk   N. English teacher

When the Legends Die Advanced Short Answer Unit Test Page 2

II. Short Answer

1. Which events in the novel are "turning points"--events which affect the course of the plot and the themes?

2. Who were Thomas' true friends? Explain your choices.

3. Discuss Thomas' growth as a person throughout the novel. What stages of growth does he go through?

4. Compare and contrast Thomas with Blue Elk.

When the Legends Die Advanced Short Answer Unit Test Page 3

5. What was the purpose of the appearance of the All-Mother?

6. Why was Meo included in the story?

7. What were the "songs"? What was their purpose?

8. Explore the role of death in the story. Compare and contrast the deaths of George, Bessie, Red Dillon, Meo, and the animals.

When the Legends Die Advanced Short Answer Unit Test Page 4

III. Composition

"When the legends die, the dreams end.
  When the dreams end, there is no more greatness."

Explain why that quotation is written at the beginning of the book *When the Legends Die*. How does it relate to the book?

When the Legends Die Advanced Short Answer Unit Test Page 5

IV. Vocabulary

Listen to the vocabulary words and write them down. After you have written down all the words, write a paragraph using all of the vocabulary words. The paragraph must in some way relate to *When the Legends Die*.

MULTIPLE CHOICE UNIT TEST 1 - *When the Legends Die*

I. Matching

___ 1. Bessie   A. Thomas' roommate

___ 2. Jim Thatcher   B. Author

___ 3. Benny Grayback   C. Nurse

___ 4. George   D. English teacher

___ 5. Hal Borland   E. Tended his beans and peppers

___ 6. Red Dillon   F. Killer Tom; Bear's Brother

___ 7. Thomas Black Bull   G. Carpentry teacher

___ 8. Rowena Ellis   H. Burned Thomas' lodge

___ 9. Luther   I. Killed Frank No Deer

___ 10. Meo   J. Owned a sheep ranch

___ 11. Neil Swanson   K. Store owner

___ 12. Albert Left Hand   L. Bet on Tom at the rodeos

___ 13. Mary Redmond   M. Bear's Brother's Mother

___ 14. Blue Elk   N. Flogged Thomas for fighting

When the Legends Die Multiple Choice Unit Test 1 Page 2

II. Multiple Choice
1. Why did George and his family go to the mountains?
    a. They were going on a fishing trip to one of George's favorite streams.
    b. George killed Frank No Deer. He and his family fled to get away from trouble.
    c. They owed money to the company store and were not able to pay. They went to the mountains to trap furs to use in exchange for payment of their debt.
    d. Bessie was sick. George knew of an old medicine man who lived alone in the mountains. He took her there hoping she would be cured.

2. Why did George kill Frank No Deer?
    a. Frank had been making advances to Bessie and George was jealous.
    b. George was drunk. They got into a fist fight about who was stronger and George beat him to death.
    c. Some of the white men wanted Frank out of the way because he was a bad influence. They offered George a large sum of money to do the job. He saw it as an opportunity to get enough money to buy his way out of the sawmill.
    d. Three different times George had saved enough money to pay off his store debt. Each time, Frank stole the money. The third time Frank stole the money, George killed him.

3. How did George die?
    a. He was killed in an avalanche while out hunting for meat.
    b. He was bitten by a rattlesnake.
    c. He stepped into a hunter's trap. He managed to get loose, but the wound got infected. Eventually he got gangrene and died.
    d. He was killed by an angry bear.

4. Why did Blue Elk go to the woods to find the boy?
    a. He was the boy's godfather, and felt it was his responsibility to protect the boy.
    b. He wanted to bring the boy home as a servant, since he had no family of his own.
    c. He wanted to live the old way with the boy.
    d. The preacher hired him to do it.

5. How did the bear's return change Thomas?
    a. He was more vocal about remembering the old ways.
    b. He was happier than he had ever been.
    c. He became very studious.
    d. He was more alone and sad than ever before.

When the Legends Die Multiple Choice Unit Test 1 Page 3

6. What did Thomas think of plowing?
    a. He enjoyed being so close to the land, getting out in the fresh air and sunshine for exercise, and having the opportunity to see things grow.
    b. He thought it was senseless to try to make the land grow something that wasn't there naturally. He thought plowing was a waste of time because you didn't go anywhere with all that walking.
    c. He liked it because it gave him time to think.
    d. He liked it because the earth gave him strength.

7. Which of the following was not part of Red's scam?
    a. He placed small bets on Thomas in the early rounds.
    b. He made Thomas lose in the finals.
    c. He told people that Tom had never ridden in a rodeo before.
    d. He talked people into setting up a special event.

8. Why did Tom have a losing streak?
    a. He was depressed about Red's death and couldn't concentrate.
    b. He was suffering from pneumonia and wasn't taking care of himself.
    c. He was just getting bad horses; there wasn't anything he could do about it.
    d. He started riding for the crowd instead of concentrating on the ride itself.

9. How did Tom feel about seeing the bear's tracks?
    a. He was glad to see that there were still bears in the area.
    b. It made him sad, because it reminded him of the bear he had as an Indian child.
    c. The tracks made him fearful.
    d. It made him angry, though his anger was misplaced just as it had been in the earlier incident with the horses.

10. Why did Tom go back to Horse Mountain to look for the bear?
    a. He wanted to kill it and make a clean break from his past.
    b. He thought it was his childhood bear. He wanted to try and tame it again.
    c. He was just curious to see if it was, indeed, the same bear he had known as a child.
    d. It had to be destroyed so it would not attack people any more. Someone had to kill it, and Tom felt a certain obligation to the task.

When the Legends Die Multiple Choice Unit Test Page 4

11. What did Tom say to the deer picture?
    a. He apologized for killing her sister and wasting the meat.
    b. He thanked the deer for the delicious meat and said he hoped she didn't feel too much pain from the bullet.
    c. He said it was the deer's lot in life to be eaten by man, who was more powerful.
    d. He said nothing. He thought the old way of talking to animal spirits was foolish.

III. Composition

When the Legends Die has been called, "An extraordinary novel about man, nature and courage. . . ." Defend this statement using examples from the novel.

When the Legends Die Multiple Choice Unit Test 1 Page 5

IV. Vocabulary: Multiple choice. Write in the letter of the definition that matches the word.

____ 1. AMBIGUOUS A. Tendons

____ 2. ZEAL B. Refusing to give up or let go

____ 3. ABASHED C. Tending to provoke; exciting; stimulating

____ 4. TACITURN D. A hole where things can be hidden

____ 5. PENANCE E. Elaborately

____ 6. STIFLE F. Tired

____ 7. RANCID G. Puzzled; perplexed; confused

____ 8. WEARY H. Hold back; suppress; repress

____ 9. TAUNTED I. Became used to a condition

____ 10. ORNATELY J. The state or act of looking forward to something

____ 11. EXPECTANCY K. Untalkative

____ 12. PLIANT L. Teased; mocked

____ 13. CACHE M. In a manner preoccupied by unwholesome matters

____ 14. ACCLIMATED N. Indefinite; open to several interpretations

____ 15. PROVOCATIVE O. Rotten

____ 16. BAFFLED P. An act done to show repentance for a wrong doing

____ 17. PERSISTENT Q. Ashamed; embarrassed

____ 18. INFURIATED R. Made very angry

____ 19. MORBIDLY S. Enthusiasm

____ 20. SINEW T. Bendable

MULTIPLE CHOICE UNIT TEST 2 - *When the Legends Die*

I. Matching

___ 1. Bessie   A. Store owner

___ 2. Jim Thatcher   B. Bet on Tom at the rodeos

___ 3. Benny Grayback   C. Bear's Brother's Mother

___ 4. George   D. Flogged Thomas for fighting

___ 5. Hal Borland   E. Killed Frank No Deer

___ 6. Red Dillon   F. Burned Thomas' lodge

___ 7. Thomas Black Bull   G. Owned a sheep ranch

___ 8. Rowena Ellis   H. Killer Tom; Bear's Brother

___ 9. Luther   I. Tended his beans and peppers

___ 10. Meo   J. Carpentry teacher

___ 11. Neil Swanson   K. Thomas' roommate

___ 12. Albert Left Hand   L. Author

___ 13. Mary Redmond   M. Nurse

___ 14. Blue Elk   N. English teacher

When the Legends Die Multiple Choice Unit Test 2 Page 2

II. Multiple Choice
1. Why did George and his family go to the mountains?
    a. Bessie was sick. George knew of an old medicine man who lived alone in the mountains. He took her there hoping she would be cured.
    b. They were going on a fishing trip to one of George's favorite streams.
    c. They owed money to the company store and were not able to pay. They went to the mountains to trap furs to use in exchange for payment of their debt.
    d. George killed Frank No Deer. He and his family fled to get away from trouble.

2. Why did George kill Frank No Deer?
    a. Three different times George had saved enough money to pay off his store debt. Each time, Frank stole the money. The third time Frank stole the money, George killed him.
    b. Some of the white men wanted Frank out of the way because he was a bad influence. They offered George a large sum of money to do the job. He saw it as an opportunity to get enough money to buy his way out of the sawmill.
    c. Frank had been making advances to Bessie and George was jealous.
    d. George was drunk. They got into a fist fight about who was stronger and George beat him to death.

3. How did George die?
    a. He was killed by an angry bear.
    b. He stepped into a hunter's trap. He managed to get loose, but the wound got infected. Eventually he got gangrene and died.
    c. He was killed in an avalanche while out hunting for meat.
    d. He was bitten by a rattlesnake.

4. Why did Blue Elk go to the woods to find the boy?
    a. He wanted to live the old way with the boy.
    b. The preacher hired him to do it.
    c. He was the boy's godfather, and felt it was his responsibility to protect the boy.
    d. He wanted to bring the boy home as a servant, since he had no family of his own.

5. How did the bear's return change Thomas?
    a. He became very studious.
    b. He was happier than he had ever been.
    c. He was more alone and sad than ever before.
    d. He was more vocal about remembering the old ways.

When the Legends Die Multiple Choice Unit Test 2 Page 3

6. What did Thomas think of plowing?
    a. He liked it because the earth gave him strength.
    b. He enjoyed being so close to the land, getting out in the fresh air and sunshine for exercise, and having the opportunity to see things grow.
    c. He liked it because it gave him time to think.
    d. He thought it was senseless to try to make the land grow something that wasn't there naturally. He thought plowing was a waste of time because you didn't go anywhere with all that walking.

7. Which of the following was not part of Red's scam?
    a. He made Thomas lose in the finals.
    b. He placed small bets on Thomas in the early rounds.
    c. He talked people into setting up a special event.
    d. He told people that Tom had never ridden in a rodeo before.

8. Why did Tom have a losing streak?
    a. He was just getting bad horses; there wasn't anything he could do about it.
    b. He started riding for the crowd instead of concentrating on the ride itself.
    c. He was depressed about Red's death and couldn't concentrate.
    d. He was suffering from pneumonia and wasn't taking care of himself.

9. How did Tom feel about seeing the bear's tracks?
    a. It made him angry, though his anger was misplaced just as it had been in the earlier incident with the horses.
    b. He was glad to see that there were still bears in the area.
    c. It made him sad, because it reminded him of the bear he had as an Indian child.
    d. The tracks made him fearful.

10. Why did Tom go back to Horse Mountain to look for the bear?
    a. It had to be destroyed so it would not attack people any more. Someone had to kill it, and Tom felt a certain obligation to the task.
    b. He was just curious to see if it was, indeed, the same bear he had known as a child.
    c. He thought it was his childhood bear. He wanted to try and tame it again.
    d. He wanted to kill it and make a clean break from his past.

When the Legends Die Multiple Choice Unit Test 2 Page 4

11. What did Tom say to the deer picture?
    a. He said nothing. He thought the old way of talking to animal spirits was foolish.
    b. He said it was the deer's lot in life to be eaten by man, who was more powerful.
    c. He apologized for killing her sister and wasting the meat.
    d. He thanked the deer for the delicious meat and said he hoped she didn't feel too much pain from the bullet.

III. Composition

Why did Tom return to the old way of life? What circumstances in his life led him to this decision?

When the Legends Die Multiple Choice Unit Test 2 Page 5

IV. Vocabulary   Match the correct definitions to the words.

____ 1. MORBIDLY   A. Untalkative

____ 2. ZEAL   B. Skillful

____ 3. ABASHED   C. Teased; mocked

____ 4. MALEVOLENT   D. Summoned by using gestures

____ 5. SATED   E. A hole where things can be hidden

____ 6. EQUILIBRIUM   F. Malicious; evil; wishing harm to others

____ 7. BAFFLED   G. Tendons

____ 8. ACCLIMATED   H. Elaborately

____ 9. DUBIOUS   I. Doubtful

____ 10. DEFT   J. Became used to a condition

____ 11. BECKONED   K. Balance

____ 12. DISCONSOLATE   L. Enthusiasm

____ 13. ORNATELY   M. Attentive; full of desire; eager

____ 14. SINEW   N. Puzzled; perplexed; confused

____ 15. TACITURN   O. Completely filled or satisfied

____ 16. CACHE   P. Gloomy; hopelessly sad

____ 17. TAUNTED   Q. Tired

____ 18. INFURIATED   R. Made very angry

____ 19. SOLICITOUS   S. In a manner preoccupied by unwholesome matters

____ 20. WEARY   T. Ashamed; embarrassed

ANSWER SHEET - *When the Legends Die*
Multiple Choice Unit Tests

I. Matching	II. Multiple Choice	IV. Vocabulary
1. ___	1. ___	1. ___
2. ___	2. ___	2. ___
3. ___	3. ___	3. ___
4. ___	4. ___	4. ___
5. ___	5. ___	5. ___
6. ___	6. ___	6. ___
7. ___	7. ___	7. ___
8. ___	8. ___	8. ___
9. ___	9. ___	9. ___
10. ___	10. ___	10. ___
11. ___	11. ___	11. ___
12. ___		12. ___
13. ___		13. ___
14. ___		14. ___
		15. ___
		16. ___
		17. ___
		18. ___
		19. ___
		20. ___

ANSWER KEY - *When the Legends Die*
Multiple Choice Unit Tests

Answers to Unit Test 1 are in the left column. Answers to Unit Test 2 are in the right column.

I. Matching	II. Multiple Choice	IV. Vocabulary
1. M C	1. B D	1. N S
2. K A	2. D A	2. S L
3. G J	3. A C	3. Q T
4. I E	4. D B	4. K F
5. B L	5. D C	5. P O
6. L B	6. B D	6. H K
7. F H	7. B A	7. O N
8. D N	8. D B	8. F J
9. A K	9. B C	9. L I
10. E I	10. A D	10. E B
11. N D	11. A C	11. J D
12. J G		12. T P
13. C M		13. D H
14. H F		14. I G
		15. C A
		16. G E
		17. B C
		18. R R
		19. M M
		20. A Q

UNIT RESOURCE MATERIALS

BULLETIN BOARD IDEAS - *When the Legends Die*

1. Save one corner of the board for the best of students' *When the Legends Die* writing assignments.

2. Take one of the word search puzzles from the extra activities section and with a marker copy it over in a large size on the bulletin board. Write the clue words to find to one side. Invite students prior to and after class to find the words and circle them on the bulletin board.

3. Title the board *When the Legends Die*: A NOVEL FULL OF CHARACTERS. Find pictures in magazines (or perhaps your library has a file of pictures) of people who look like the various characters in the novel. Place the picture on colorful paper, write the character's name under the picture (or next to it) and write a brief description of the character by it. You may wish to arrange these pictures on a genealogical table to show the relationships among the characters.

4. Write several of the most significant quotations from the book onto the board on brightly colored paper.

5. Make a bulletin board listing the vocabulary words for this unit. As you complete sections of the novel and discuss the vocabulary for each section, write the definitions on the bulletin board. (If your board is one students face frequently, it will help them learn the words.)

6. Place a map of the United States on the board and mark all of the places where Tom traveled to ride in rodeos.

7. Make a bulletin board about North American Indians, showing on a map where various tribes were located.

8. Do a bulletin board about survival skills, giving important tips about staying alive in the wild.

9. Do a bulletin board about "heritage." Have your students bring in pictures which represent their own heritages, the backgrounds of their ancestors. As an introductory activity, have each student post his/her picture(s) on the board and tell a little about his/her family history.

10. Make a bulletin board about legends on which you post students' written summaries of the legends they researched.

11. Make a bulletin board about "Indian Lore," facts about the customs of various tribes of Indians.

EXTRA ACTIVITIES - *When the Legends Die*

One of the difficulties in teaching a novel is that all students don't read at the same speed. One student who likes to read may take the book home and finish it in a day or two. Sometimes a few students finish the in-class assignments early. The problem, then, is finding suitable extra activities for students.

One thing you can do is to keep a little library in the classroom. For this unit on *When the Legends Die*, biographical information about Hal Borland would be interesting for some students. You can include other related books and articles about Native Americans, fishing, camping, survival skills, farming, rodeos, riding , horses, physical therapy, gardening, or critics' articles about *When the Legends Die*. Information about careers in education, farming, raising livestock, medicine, business or the natural sciences might also be appropriate.

Other things you may keep on hand are puzzles. We have made some relating directly to *When the Legends Die* for you. Feel free to duplicate them.

Some students may like to draw. You might devise a contest or allow some extra-credit grade for students who draw characters or scenes from *When the Legends Die*. Note, too, that if the students do not want to keep their drawings you may pick up some extra bulletin board materials this way. If you have a contest and you supply the prize (a CD or something like that perhaps), you could, possibly, make the drawing itself a non-returnable entry fee.

The pages which follow contain games, puzzles and worksheets. The keys, when appropriate, immediately follow the puzzle or worksheet. There are two main groups of activities: one group for the unit; that is, generally relating to the *When the Legends Die* text, and another group of activities related strictly to the *When the Legends Die* vocabulary.

Directions for these games, puzzles and worksheets are self-explanatory. The object here is to provide you with extra materials you may use in any way you choose.

MORE ACTIVITIES - *When the Legends Die*

1. Pick a chapter or scene with a great deal of dialogue and have the students act it out on a stage. (Perhaps you could assign various scenes to different groups of students so more than one scene could be acted and more students could participate.)

2. Use some of the related topics (noted earlier for an in-class library) as topics for research, reports or written papers, or as topics for guest speakers.

3. Take short scenes from the novel. Assign parts in the scenes to various students (so that each student has a part). Students should memorize their lines and dress up as their characters to perform their scenes in front of the class in your classroom or on stage.

4. Have students design a book cover (front and back and inside flaps) for *When the Legends Die*.

5. Have students design a bulletin board (ready to be put up; not just sketched) for *When the Legends Die*.

6. Take a trip to (or watch a documentary about) rodeo riding. This is also a fun introductory activity.

7. Have each student or pairs of students research and report on one North American Indian tribe, including history, culture, ceremonies, current status, etc.

8. Have your students write words to the "songs" which are mentioned in the story.

9. Have each student complete a project related to the story: basket weaving, making an article of clothing, learning to shoot a bow and arrow, etc.

10. Have your students write "songs" appropriate for our modern day lives.

11. Hold a discussion about ways we do not live in harmony with nature. Explore the benefits and drawbacks of our society today.

12. Thomas spent a great deal of time trying to answer the question, "Who am I?" Give your students time to try to answer that question for themselves. They could write a composition, or make a mural or a video.

WORD SEARCH - *When the Legends Die*

All words in this list are associated with *When the Legends Die*. The words are placed backwards, forward, diagonally, up and down. The included words are listed below the word searches.

```
A V A L A N C H E K N N V S R F W M F L D H J X
G M W N F Z S L C O R R W W F G H X E G Q Q P H
Z R X Z P F M S I R G Z H C R S N P B A L R S S
L J A M F M D T F G E M Q F B L A N K E T S D W
Y P Y Y Z C A Y K J D H C M S S W W V R H N J H
R F S D B V R P D X Q H T C Z T W B A G A E D Q
L L K Q R A W O Y S H M Y U H A C I R L R L X R
E L K E Y H C N W K T R E B L A L R R O W E N A
B X S L L F N K N O R A R C M K P O T E T L Q S
P E S X A E K I O B J E B P V G B S J M D H A B
R E E D B W F F U T E I D K M H T Y H R F M E O
M E P S N E R T W U T S M M B A W H A Y O A F R
R R H L P E J F L T S S S J O Q R W M H N O C J
G A X C V U G B Q S C C W I H N D Y T S M Q M N
J S I A T Q R E B L A C K P E O D B E R R I E S
Y R E N L A D S L W H W S Q O G Y M G L I W C
S B M M R T H Q H J B L M W P B R H J Q L X T D
J A R R O W S T R N O L L I D T U O P M C U B Q
W X Q R Z F F S C R K E J T L X X L E B X B K D
P E R M I T S V J S G M Z X Q L T G L G W D J Y
```

ALBERT	BULL	LEG	ROWENA
ARROWS	CAMP	LEGENDS	SAWMILL
AVALANCHE	CHAPS	LUTHER	SPURS
BEANS	CLAW	MARY	STAB
BEAVERFOOT	CUB	MEAT	STORE
BENNY	DEER	MEO	THATCHER
BERRIES	DILLON	NEIL	THOMAS
BESSIE	DOC	PERMITS	TRAIL
BIT	ELK	RAIN	UTE
BLACK	GEORGE	RED	WALK
BLANKET	GRAYBACK	REDMOND	WOODWARD
BLUE	JIM	RESERVATION	
BORLAND	KNIFE	RHYTHM	
BROTHER	LEFT	ROOM	

KEY: WORD SEARCH - *When the Legends Die*

All words in this list are associated with *When the Legends Die*. The words are placed backwards, forward, diagonally, up and down. The included words are listed below the word searches.

```
        A V A L A N C H E     N                         M
      G                         O                       E
        R                   I R                         A
          A           T       E         B L A N K E T   D
            Y       A           H                   R   N
              B V     D       T C     W B A       A E
              R A   O Y S         U H A C I R L R
      E L K E       C N   K T R E B L A L   R O W E N A
            S L L   N K N O R A   C M   P O T E T       S
            E S   A E   I O B J E B P     B S     D H A B
    R E E D B W F F U T E I D     M H T Y H R     M E O
        E   S N E R T   U T S M M     A     A O A     R
      R H   P E       L         S   O   R W   H N O
        A   C V U G B     S         I   N D Y T S       M N
          I A T   R E B L A C K   E O D B E R R I E S
            E N   A S L     W         O G               I
          B       H               M W   B R         L
          A R R O W S T     N O L L I D   U O       C U B
                              E       L       L E
          P E R M I T S         G           L     L G
```

ALBERT	BULL	LEG	ROWENA
ARROWS	CAMP	LEGENDS	SAWMILL
AVALANCHE	CHAPS	LUTHER	SPURS
BEANS	CLAW	MARY	STAB
BEAVERFOOT	CUB	MEAT	STORE
BENNY	DEER	MEO	THATCHER
BERRIES	DILLON	NEIL	THOMAS
BESSIE	DOC	PERMITS	TRAIL
BIT	ELK	RAIN	UTE
BLACK	GEORGE	RED	WALK
BLANKET	GRAYBACK	REDMOND	WOODWARD
BLUE	JIM	RESERVATION	
BORLAND	KNIFE	RHYTHM	
BROTHER	LEFT	ROOM	

CROSSWORD - *When the Legends Die*

CROSSWORD CLUES - *When the Legends Die*

ACROSS
1. Bessie bought Thomas a red one
4. Carpentry teacher
7. Bucks and does
8. ____ Elk
9. Bet on Tom
10. Black _____
11. Albert _____ Hand
12. Cowboy head cover; ten-gallon, for example
13. Bear's Brother's mother
15. Short for doctor
17. Present plural form of 'to be'
18. Bows shoot them
21. Tended his beans and peppers
23. Cowboy's night stop
26. Deer family member
27. Area from thigh to foot; Thomas broke his
28. Thomas' roommate
29. Nurse Redmond
30. One from a bear is long and sharp
32. Food from animals
34. Home; place where one lives
35. Thomas was from this Indian tribe
37. Luther and Thomas shared one
39. English teacher
42. Thomas became ___ as a rodeo rider; well-known
43. Dolly
46. Path; place where animal was
47. Mr. Left Hand
48. Each horse had his own; beat
51. Belonging to me
52. Footwear used to urge on horses
53. Benny's last name
54. Papers granting permission

DOWN
1. Author
2. Coordinating conjunction
3. Bessie bought one for Thomas
4. Bear's _____ (Thomas)
5. Flogged Thomas for fighting
6. Baby bear
7. Red's last name
8. Metal object in horse's mouth
10. Pick and eat them
13. Thomas _____ Bull
14. Some Indians were stuck working there
16. When the ___ Die
18. George was killed by one
19. Water falling from the sky
20. Tom had to learn to do it again
22. He killed Frank No Deer
24. Pierce flesh with a sharp object
25. Store owner
30. Cowboy leg protectors
31. Tom worked for him after the accident
33. Jim owned one
36. Jim's last name
38. Repast; food; eat a ____
40. High ____; twelve o'clock
41. Acquired
43. Meo grew them
44. Prefer
45. Killer Tom; Bear's Brother
49. Attempt
50. Quickly move on foot

CROSSWORD ANSWER KEY - *When the Legends Die*

MATCHING QUIZ/WORKSHEET 1 - *When the Legends Die*

___	1. SAWMILL	A. Baby bear
___	2. CUB	B. Benny's last name
___	3. ALBERT	C. Carpentry teacher
___	4. GRAYBACK	D. Where the Indians lived
___	5. BORLAND	E. Deer family member
___	6. BENNY	F. Some Indians were stuck working there
___	7. THATCHER	G. Food from animals
___	8. JIM	H. Tom worked for him after the accident
___	9. CLAW	I. Tom had to learn to do it again
___	10. RESERVATION	J. Store owner
___	11. KNIFE	K. One from a bear is long and sharp
___	12. BEAVERFOOT	L. Mr. Left Hand
___	13. MEAT	M. Bessie bought one for Thomas
___	14. WOODWARD	N. Jim's last name
___	15. DILLON	O. Dolly
___	16. WALK	P. Author
___	17. BROTHER	Q. Meo grew them
___	18. BEANS	R. Bear's _____ (Thomas)
___	19. ELK	S. Black _____
___	20. BULL	T. Red's last name

KEY: MATCHING QUIZ/WORKSHEET 1 - *When the Legends Die*

_F_	1. SAWMILL	A.	Baby bear
_A_	2. CUB	B.	Benny's last name
_L_	3. ALBERT	C.	Carpentry teacher
_B_	4. GRAYBACK	D.	Where the Indians lived
_P_	5. BORLAND	E.	Deer family member
_C_	6. BENNY	F.	Some Indians were stuck working there
_N_	7. THATCHER	G.	Food from animals
_J_	8. JIM	H.	Tom worked for him after the accident
_K_	9. CLAW	I.	Tom had to learn to do it again
_D_	10. RESERVATION	J.	Store owner
_M_	11. KNIFE	K.	One from a bear is long and sharp
_O_	12. BEAVERFOOT	L.	Mr. Left Hand
_G_	13. MEAT	M.	Bessie bought one for Thomas
_H_	14. WOODWARD	N.	Jim's last name
_T_	15. DILLON	O.	Dolly
_I_	16. WALK	P.	Author
_R_	17. BROTHER	Q.	Meo grew them
_Q_	18. BEANS	R.	Bear's _____ (Thomas)
_E_	19. ELK	S.	Black _____
_S_	20. BULL	T.	Red's last name

MATCHING QUIZ/WORKSHEET 2 - *When the Legends Die*

____ 1. LEG   A. Papers granting permission

____ 2. THATCHER   B. Tom worked for him after the accident

____ 3. BERRIES   C. Some Indians were stuck working there

____ 4. DILLON   D. Cowboy's night stop

____ 5. PERMITS   E. Bessie bought Thomas a red one

____ 6. SAWMILL   F. Nurse Mary

____ 7. BLUE   G. Meo grew them

____ 8. REDMOND   H. Red's last name

____ 9. CUB   I. Area from thigh to foot; Thomas broke his

____ 10. CAMP   J. Thomas ____ Bull

____ 11. KNIFE   K. Food from animals

____ 12. GRAYBACK   L. Pick and eat them

____ 13. BLACK   M. Bet on Tom

____ 14. RED   N. Benny's last name

____ 15. CLAW   O. ____ Elk

____ 16. BLANKET   P. Bessie bought one for Thomas

____ 17. BEANS   Q. Jim's last name

____ 18. WOODWARD   R. Baby bear

____ 19. SPURS   S. Footwear used to urge on horses

____ 20. MEAT   T. One from a bear is long and sharp

KEY: MATCHING QUIZ/WORKSHEET 2 - *When the Legends Die*

_I_	1. LEG	A. Papers granting permission
_Q_	2. THATCHER	B. Tom worked for him after the accident
_L_	3. BERRIES	C. Some Indians were stuck working there
_H_	4. DILLON	D. Cowboy's night stop
_A_	5. PERMITS	E. Bessie bought Thomas a red one
_C_	6. SAWMILL	F. Nurse Mary
_O_	7. BLUE	G. Meo grew them
_F_	8. REDMOND	H. Red's last name
_R_	9. CUB	I. Area from thigh to foot; Thomas broke his
_D_	10. CAMP	J. Thomas _____ Bull
_P_	11. KNIFE	K. Food from animals
_N_	12. GRAYBACK	L. Pick and eat them
_J_	13. BLACK	M. Bet on Tom
_M_	14. RED	N. Benny's last name
_T_	15. CLAW	O. ____ Elk
_E_	16. BLANKET	P. Bessie bought one for Thomas
_G_	17. BEANS	Q. Jim's last name
_B_	18. WOODWARD	R. Baby bear
_S_	19. SPURS	S. Footwear used to urge on horses
_K_	20. MEAT	T. One from a bear is long and sharp

JUGGLE LETTER REVIEW GAME CLUE SHEET - *When the Legends Die*

SCRAMBLED	WORD	CLUE
TLEBRA	ALBERT	Mr. Left Hand
RSAWOR	ARROWS	Bows shoot them
ACAVHELAN	AVALANCHE	George was killed by one
SABNE	BEANS	Meo grew them
OVERTOAEFB	BEAVERFOOT	Dolly
NYEBN	BENNY	Carpentry teacher
RSEERIB	BERRIES	Pick and eat them
ISEBSE	BESSIE	Bear's Brother's mother
TIB	BIT	Metal object in horse's mouth
BKLCA	BLACK	Thomas _____ Bull
KLBATEN	BLANKET	Bessie bought Thomas a red one
UBEL	BLUE	_____ Elk
DORNBAL	BORLAND	Author
HRORBTE	BROTHER	Bear's _____ (Thomas)
LUBL	BULL	Black _____
MACP	CAMP	Cowboy's night stop
HPCSA	CHAPS	Cowboy leg protectors
WLAC	CLAW	One from a bear is long and sharp
UCB	CUB	Baby bear
ERED	DEER	Bucks and does
LONLID	DILLON	Red's last name
CDO	DOC	Short for doctor
KLE	ELK	Deer family member
REGGOE	GEORGE	He killed Frank No Deer
ABKRGACY	GRAYBACK	Benny's last name
MJI	JIM	Store owner
FKEIN	KNIFE	Bessie bought one for Thomas
FELT	LEFT	Albert _____ Hand
GLE	LEG	Area from thigh to foot; Thomas broke his
NEESGLD	LEGENDS	When the ___ Die
RUTHEL	LUTHER	Thomas' roommate
RYAM	MARY	Nurse Redmond
TEAM	MEAT	Food from animals
EOM	MEO	Tended his beans and peppers
ELNI	NEIL	Flogged Thomas for fighting
STERPIM	PERMITS	Papers granting permission

Legends Clue Sheet Continued

NAIR	RAIN	Water falling from the sky
DER	RED	Bet on Tom
MODDERN	REDMOND	Nurse Mary
ONAVSRETIRE	RESERVATION	Where the Indians lived
HTMRYH	RHYTHM	Each horse had his own; beat
MORO	ROOM	Luther and Thomas shared one
ANOWER	ROWENA	English teacher
LIWMALS	SAWMILL	Some Indians were stuck working there
RPUSS	SPURS	Footwear used to urge on horses
BAST	STAB	Pierce flesh with a sharp object
RSOET	STORE	Jim owned one
CHAERTTH	THATCHER	Jim's last name
SOHMAT	THOMAS	Killer Tom; Bear's Brother
ARLTI	TRAIL	Path; place where animal was
TUE	UTE	Thomas was from this Indian tribe
KAWL	WALK	Tom had to learn to do it again
DOWRAWOD	WOODWARD	Tom worked for him after the accident

VOCABULARY RESOURCE MATERIALS

VOCABULARY WORD SEARCH - *When the Legends Die*

All words in this list are associated with *When the Legends Die* with an emphasis on the vocabulary words chosen for study in the text. The words are placed backwards, forward, diagonally, up and down. The included words are listed below.

```
L K P F T M Q R F A W S S P S L S P F L Z Z D R
D E R I S I O N A M B I G U O U S P L U M E S H
T K V E N A D R K N N A B N O R L W S I X L A N
M Z D E M I T R B E C N S I I T N L X P A W R L
L C K S R N O E W I Z I B H B V I A E I D N Y K
B E E C N E A N D H D U D Y E D I C T N B T T M
D Z A V B S D N E X D L Q E E D T N I E I H T R
C E T C I V S Z T D D D Y T Q A E Y N L L M B D
P U R T H T A C I T U R N K N U E L I O O Y I F
Z E F I I E A K C L Z U B C Q C I B F H C S M C
F E R F S N D C F J A S Y E N W A L T F C Z D B
D D L S E I P L O T F L S A C T E A I O A E J W
P E B L I D V P B V V N N H I K F A N B H B Q F
F Q L R G S J E F Z O E T V G R O S R C R Y V X
R M Z G T N T P L C P R E L Z Z O N A Y T I G V
J D F K G L Y E N Y J N P J T L M C E H S H U L
Z X J R R A P I N Q I X Z N A J H G P D F K D M
H D S N J S H H V T Y D E T A I R U F N I X H G
M X L Z N M P D H Z W R E K Q C M C J X Z G W N
V M A L E V O L E N T A C C L I M A T E D Y D L
```

ABASHED	DERISIVELY	LEVERED	REMNANT
ACCLIMATED	DISCONSOLATE	MALEVOLENT	SATED
ACRID	DUBIOUS	MORBIDLY	SINEW
AMBIGUOUS	EQUILIBRIUM	ORNATELY	SOLICITOUS
BAFFLED	EXPECTANCY	PENANCE	STIFLE
BECKONED	FATHOM	PERSISTENT	SULLEN
CACHE	HAGGLED	PINIONED	TACITURN
CONNIVING	INCONSEQUENTIALS	PLIANT	TAUNTED
CUFFED	INEVITABILITY	PLUME	WEARY
DEFT	INFURIATED	PROVOCATIVE	ZEAL
DERISION	LEACHED	RANCID	

KEY: VOCABULARY WORD SEARCH - *When the Legends Die*

All words in this list are associated with *When the Legends Die* with an emphasis on the vocabulary words chosen for study in the text. The words are placed backwards, forward, diagonally, up and down. The included words are listed below.

```
        L     P     M     R     A           S     S     S  P           Z
        D  E  R  I  S  I  O  N  A  M  B  I  G  U  O  U  S  P  L  U  M  E  S
           V  E  N  A  D  R     N  N  A     N  O  R  L        I  X  L  A
              E  M  I  T     B  E  C     S  I  I  T  N  L     P  A        L
        L     R  N  O  E  W  I     I  B  H     V  I  A  E  I     N  Y
           E  E  C     E  A  N  D     D  U  D     E  D  I  C  T  N     T  T
        D     A  V        D  N  E     D  L     E  E  D  T  N  I  E  I
        C  E     C  I     S  T  D        Y  T  Q  A  E     N  L  L  M     D
        P  U  R  T  H  T  A  C  I  T  U  R  N     N  U  E  L  I  O  O  Y  I
              E  F  I  I  E  A           U  B  C  Q  C  I  B  F  H  C  S
              E  R  F  S     D  C        A     Y  E  N  W  A  L  T  F  C
        D     L  S  E  I        O  T        S  A  C  T  E  A  I  O  A  E
              E     I  D  V        V     N  N     I  K  F  A  N  B  H  B
                 L        S     E        O  E     V        O  S  R  C  R
                    G        T     L  C  P  R  E           O  N  A  Y     I
                       G        E  N  Y     N  P        L     C  E        U
                          A     I  N     I           A              D     M
                             H        T     D  E  T  A  I  R  U  F  N  I
                                               E
                 M  A  L  E  V  O  L  E  N  T  A  C  C  L  I  M  A  T  E  D
```

ABASHED	DERISIVELY	LEVERED	REMNANT
ACCLIMATED	DISCONSOLATE	MALEVOLENT	SATED
ACRID	DUBIOUS	MORBIDLY	SINEW
AMBIGUOUS	EQUILIBRIUM	ORNATELY	SOLICITOUS
BAFFLED	EXPECTANCY	PENANCE	STIFLE
BECKONED	FATHOM	PERSISTENT	SULLEN
CACHE	HAGGLED	PINIONED	TACITURN
CONNIVING	INCONSEQUENTIALS	PLIANT	TAUNTED
CUFFED	INEVITABILITY	PLUME	WEARY
DEFT	INFURIATED	PROVOCATIVE	ZEAL
DERISION	LEACHED	RANCID	

VOCABULARY CROSSWORD - *When the Legends Die*

VOCABULARY CROSSWORD CLUES - *When the Legends Die*

ACROSS
- 3. A hole where things can be hidden
- 5. Summoned by using gestures
- 8. Water falling from the sky
- 9. Deer family member
- 10. Puzzled; perplexed; confused
- 14. Either's partner
- 17. Rotten
- 18. Area from thigh to foot; Thomas broke his
- 19. Slapped
- 21. Pierce flesh with a sharp object
- 22. Tendons
- 23. A smell
- 24. Hold back; suppress; repress
- 26. Store owner
- 27. Dusty earth
- 28. The horses had to be ___; given food
- 29. Enthusiasm
- 32. Harsh to the taste or smell
- 35. Bet on Tom
- 36. Short for doctor
- 37. Bendable
- 38. Sulky; moody
- 40. A feather-like form, structure or object
- 42. Thomas was from this Indian tribe
- 43. Bessie bought one for Thomas
- 44. Rafter
- 47. Sight organ
- 48. Ashamed; embarrassed
- 50. He killed Frank No Deer
- 52. Something left over
- 55. The state or act of looking forward to something
- 57. Food from animals

DOWN
- 1. Bows shoot them
- 2. Metal object in horse's mouth
- 4. Indefinite; open to several interpretations
- 6. Baby bear
- 7. Ridicule; scoffing; mocking
- 11. Understand; believe
- 12. Balance
- 13. Bargained; argued over terms
- 15. Mr. Left Hand
- 16. Skillful
- 20. Belittling; making less of something
- 25. Made very angry
- 27. In a scoffing or ridiculing manner
- 30. Removed soluble parts by running through a substance
- 31. ____ Elk
- 32. Became used to a condition
- 33. Completely filled or satisfied
- 34. Thomas ____ Bull
- 39. Pushed as if using a lever
- 41. An act done to show repentance for a wrong doing
- 45. Cowboy's night stop
- 46. Tended his beans and peppers
- 49. Ingest food
- 51. Luther and Thomas shared one
- 53. Nurse Redmond
- 54. Coordinating conjunction
- 56. Affirmative reply

VOCABULARY CROSSWORD ANSWER KEY - *When the Legends Die*

VOCABULARY WORKSHEET 1 - *When the Legends Die*

____ 1. Pushed as if using a lever
    A. Levered   B. Stifle   C. Deft   D. Sated

____ 2. Restrained by restricting one's arms
    A. Weary   B. Disconsolate   C. Pinioned   D. Acclimated

____ 3. Became used to a condition
    A. Solicitous   B. Ambiguous   C. Acclimated   D. Sated

____ 4. Bargained; argued over terms
    A. Fathom   B. Ambiguous   C. Plume   D. Haggled

____ 5. Untalkative
    A. Taciturn   B. Remnant   C. Solicitous   D. Persistent

____ 6. Sulky; moody
    A. Conniving   B. Disconsolate   C. Provocative   D. Sullen

____ 7. Belittling; making less of something
    A. Depreciating   B. Deft   C. Provocative   D. Baffled

____ 8. Things that don't matter or don't have significance
    A. Depreciating   B. Acclimated   C. Inconsequentials   D. Sinew

____ 9. The state or act of looking forward to something
    A. Expectancy   B. Equilibrium   C. Derisively   D. Penance

____ 10. Understand; believe
    A. Ornately   B. Derision   C. Taunted   D. Fathom

____ 11. In a manner preoccupied by unwholesome matters
    A. Leached   B. Fathom   C. Morbidly   D. Haggled

____ 12. Summoned by using gestures
    A. Zeal   B. Pliant   C. Beckoned   D. Ambiguous

____ 13. Conspiring; pretending ignorance of a wrong
    A. Stifle   B. Sinew   C. Pinioned   D. Conniving

____ 14. Refusing to give up or let go
    A. Infuriated   B. Persistent   C. Baffled   D. Zeal

____ 15. Indefinite; open to several interpretations
    A. Ambiguous   B. Zeal   C. Inconsequentials   D. Solicitous

____ 16. Doubtful
    A. Pinioned   B. Disconsolate   C. Dubious   D. Zeal

____ 17. Balance
    A. Equilibrium   B. Ambiguous   C. Ornately   D. Penance

____ 18. Hold back; suppress; repress
    A. Pinioned   B. Leached   C. Deft   D. Stifle

____ 19. Tendons
    A. Sinew   B. Baffled   C. Deft   D. Beckoned

____ 20. Puzzled; perplexed; confused
    A. Conniving   B. Remnant   C. Baffled   D. Sinew

KEY: VOCABULARY WORKSHEET 1 - *When the Legends Die*

_A_ 1. Pushed as if using a lever
    A. Levered   B. Stifle   C. Deft   D. Sated

_C_ 2. Restrained by restricting one's arms
    A. Weary   B. Disconsolate   C. Pinioned   D. Acclimated

_C_ 3. Became used to a condition
    A. Solicitous   B. Ambiguous   C. Acclimated   D. Sated

_D_ 4. Bargained; argued over terms
    A. Fathom   B. Ambiguous   C. Plume   D. Haggled

_A_ 5. Untalkative
    A. Taciturn   B. Remnant   C. Solicitous   D. Persistent

_D_ 6. Sulky; moody
    A. Conniving   B. Disconsolate   C. Provocative   D. Sullen

_A_ 7. Belittling; making less of something
    A. Depreciating   B. Deft   C. Provocative   D. Baffled

_C_ 8. Things that don't matter or don't have significance
    A. Depreciating   B. Acclimated   C. Inconsequentials   D. Sinew

_A_ 9. The state or act of looking forward to something
    A. Expectancy   B. Equilibrium   C. Derisively   D. Penance

_D_ 10. Understand; believe
    A. Ornately   B. Derision   C. Taunted   D. Fathom

_C_ 11. In a manner preoccupied by unwholesome matters
    A. Leached   B. Fathom   C. Morbidly   D. Haggled

_C_ 12. Summoned by using gestures
    A. Zeal   B. Pliant   C. Beckoned   D. Ambiguous

_D_ 13. Conspiring; pretending ignorance of a wrong
    A. Stifle   B. Sinew   C. Pinioned   D. Conniving

_B_ 14. Refusing to give up or let go
    A. Infuriated   B. Persistent   C. Baffled   D. Zeal

_A_ 15. Indefinite; open to several interpretations
    A. Ambiguous   B. Zeal   C. Inconsequentials   D. Solicitous

_C_ 16. Doubtful
    A. Pinioned   B. Disconsolate   C. Dubious   D. Zeal

_A_ 17. Balance
    A. Equilibrium   B. Ambiguous   C. Ornately   D. Penance

_D_ 18. Hold back; suppress; repress
    A. Pinioned   B. Leached   C. Deft   D. Stifle

_A_ 19. Tendons
    A. Sinew   B. Baffled   C. Deft   D. Beckoned

_C_ 20. Puzzled; perplexed; confused
    A. Conniving   B. Remnant   C. Baffled   D. Sinew

VOCABULARY WORKSHEET 2 - *When the Legends Die*

_____ 1. PINIONED   A. Understand; believe

_____ 2. TACITURN   B. Tendons

_____ 3. SINEW   C. In a scoffing or ridiculing manner

_____ 4. EXPECTANCY   D. Untalkative

_____ 5. DERISION   E. In a manner preoccupied by unwholesome matters

_____ 6. RANCID   F. Belittling; making less of something

_____ 7. LEACHED   G. A hole where things can be hidden

_____ 8. FATHOM   H. Restrained by restricting one's arms

_____ 9. BAFFLED   I. Quality of not being able to be avoided

_____ 10. PLUME   J. Skillful

_____ 11. STIFLE   K. Rotten

_____ 12. CACHE   L. Ridicule; scoffing; mocking

_____ 13. INEVITABILITY   M. A feather-like form, structure or object

_____ 14. DEFT   N. The state or act of looking forward to something

_____ 15. EQUILIBRIUM   O. Removed soluble parts by running through a substance

_____ 16. REMNANT   P. Puzzled; perplexed; confused

_____ 17. INCONSEQUENTIALS Q. Hold back; suppress; repress

_____ 18. MORBIDLY   R. Something left over

_____ 19. DEPRECIATING   S. Things that don't matter or don't have significance

_____ 20. DERISIVELY   T. Balance

KEY: VOCABULARY WORKSHEET 2 - *When the Legends Die*

H	1. PINIONED	A.	Understand; believe
D	2. TACITURN	B.	Tendons
B	3. SINEW	C.	In a scoffing or ridiculing manner
N	4. EXPECTANCY	D.	Untalkative
L	5. DERISION	E.	In a manner preoccupied by unwholesome matters
K	6. RANCID	F.	Belittling; making less of something
O	7. LEACHED	G.	A hole where things can be hidden
A	8. FATHOM	H.	Restrained by restricting one's arms
P	9. BAFFLED	I.	Quality of not being able to be avoided
M	10. PLUME	J.	Skillful
Q	11. STIFLE	K.	Rotten
G	12. CACHE	L.	Ridicule; scoffing; mocking
I	13. INEVITABILITY	M.	A feather-like form, structure or object
J	14. DEFT	N.	The state or act of looking forward to something
T	15. EQUILIBRIUM	O.	Removed soluble parts by running through a substance
R	16. REMNANT	P.	Puzzled; perplexed; confused
S	17. INCONSEQUENTIALS	Q.	Hold back; suppress; repress
E	18. MORBIDLY	R.	Something left over
F	19. DEPRECIATING	S.	Things that don't matter or don't have significance
C	20. DERISIVELY	T.	Balance

VOCABULARY JUGGLE LETTER REVIEW GAME CLUES - *When the Legends Die*

SCRAMBLED	WORD	CLUE
SEDHABA	ABASHED	Ashamed; embarrassed
CAMDACLETI	ACCLIMATED	Became used to a condition
RADIC	ACRID	Harsh to the taste or smell
BOSAMGIUU	AMBIGUOUS	Indefinite; open to several interpretations
FADFEBL	BAFFLED	Puzzled; perplexed; confused
ONBCEDEK	BECKONED	Summoned by using gestures
HACCE	CACHE	A hole where things can be hidden
INGONNCIV	CONNIVING	Conspiring; pretending ignorance of a wrong
FUDCEF	CUFFED	Slapped
TEDF	DEFT	Skillful
CATPERNIDGEI	DEPRECIATING	Belittling; making less of something
IROSNEDI	DERISION	Ridicule; scoffing; mocking
RYSILVEEDI	DERISIVELY	In a scoffing or ridiculing manner
TASODOSECLIN	DISCONSOLATE	Gloomy; hopelessly sad
SUUDBIO	DUBIOUS	Doubtful
IQIMUERBILU	EQUILIBRIUM	Balance
TEXEPACCYN	EXPECTANCY	The state or act of looking forward to something
HAMFOT	FATHOM	Understand; believe
GLADHEG	HAGGLED	Bargained; argued over terms
LIVINATTYIBIE	INEVITABILITY	Quality of not being able to be avoided
AFEDNUTIRI	INFURIATED	Made very angry
HEEDLAC	LEACHED	Removed soluble parts by running through a substance
REELVED	LEVERED	Pushed as if using a lever
TLEEVLOMAN	MALEVOLENT	Malicious; evil; wishing harm to others
BRIMDYLO	MORBIDLY	In a manner preoccupied by unwholesome matters
NYRETOLA	ORNATELY	Elaborately
CANNEEP	PENANCE	An act done to show repentance for a wrong doing
TRESSPINET	PERSISTENT	Refusing to give up or let go
INDONEPI	PINIONED	Restrained by restricting one's arms
TLANIP	PLIANT	Bendable
UMPEL	PLUME	A feather-like form, structure or object
IVOVOTREPCA	PROVOCATIVE	Tending to provoke; exciting; stimulating
RIDNAC	RANCID	Rotten
TANNMER	REMNANT	Something left over
DATES	SATED	Completely filled or satisfied
WINES	SINEW	Tendons
CUTILOOSSI	SOLICITOUS	Attentive; full of desire; eager

www.ingramcontent.com/pod-product-compliance
Lightning Source LLC
Chambersburg PA
CBHW051415070526
44584CB00023B/3434